D0086539

LOREN EISELEY

Literature and Life series
(Formerly Modern Literature and World Dramatists)

GENERAL EDITOR: *Philip Winsor*

Selected list of titles:

Complete list of titles in the series available from publisher on request.

PS 3555 .I78 Z67 1983
Gerber, Leslie E.
Loren Eiseley /

LOREN EISELEY

Leslie E. Gerber
Margaret McFadden

Frederick Ungar Publishing Co.
New York

RITTER LIBRARY
BALDWIN-WALLACE COLLEGE
WITHDRAWN

Copyright © 1983 by Frederick Ungar Publishing Co., Inc.
Printed in the United States of America

Lines from Loren Eiseley, *The Innocent Assassins*.
Copyright © 1973 by Loren Eiseley (New York: Charles
Scribner's Sons, 1973). Reprinted with the permission of
Charles Scribner's Sons.
Lines from Loren Eiseley, *Another Kind of Autumn*.
Copyright © 1976, 1977 by the Estate of Loren Eiseley
(New York: Charles Scribner's Sons, 1977). Reprinted with
the permission of Charles Scribner's Sons.

Library of Congress Cataloging in Publication Data

Gerber, Leslie E.
  Loren Eiseley.

  (Literature and life series)
  Bibliography: p.
  Includes index.
  1. Eiseley, Loren C., 1907-1977—Criticism and
interpretation.   I. McFadden, Margaret.   II. Title.
III. Series.
PS3555.I78Z67   1983   818'.5409   82-40294
ISBN 0-8044-5424-8

Acknowledgments

Many people and several institutions have helped us write this book. Our thanks are offered to all, both those we note and those not mentioned by name. At the University of Pennsylvania's anthropology department, professors Ben Reina and Ward Goodenough offered many hours of time, as did Jeanne Gallagher, departmental secretary. The professionals at Penn's archives and library were extremely helpful during our stay. Ms. Caroline Werkley, Eiseley's assistant, now of Moberly, Missouri, answered many telephone queries. The Rev. John McEllhenny of the Ardmore (Pa.) Methodist Church generously shared reminiscences. Mrs. Mabel Eiseley of Wynnewood, Pennsylvania, has been most gracious in responding to questions.

We want to thank the Graduate School of Appalachian State University for a grant to help with the typing costs. For her accurate, efficient typing we are indebted to Ms. Marsha Turner. The coordinator of Interdisciplinary Studies at Appalachian State University, Peter Petschauer, deserves special mention for securing some released time for us during the spring of 1980.

Lastly and perhaps most importantly we want to thank especially our various childcare givers—from California to Pennsylvania and from Oshkosh to Boone—who enabled us to research and write this book while our daughter was between nine months and three years old.

For Phil Windrem
and
Lina Mainiero

Contents

Chronology

1907 Loren Corey Eiseley born in Lincoln, Nebraska, September 3. Son of Clyde Edwin and Daisy Corey Eiseley; only sibling a half-brother, Leo, fourteen years older.

1912 Nebraska prison escape and subsequent shooting of Tom Murry, symbolic public event in Eiseley's early life.

1913 Writes first book, *Animal Aventures* [sic], a pencilled manuscript.

1910–1920 Frequent family moves in Nebraska; interest in skull collection in university museum and in biology.

1921–1924 High school in Lincoln; "I want to be a nature writer," he writes in English essay.

1924 Graduation from high school, Lincoln; enrolls at University of Nebraska.

1927 Publishes first piece in *The Prairie Schooner*.

1928 Joins staff of *The Prairie Schooner* as an editor. Father dies of cancer at age 60; Eiseley drops out of school.
Tuberculosis diagnosed, goes to Colorado for "cure," returns to Lincoln, still ill.

1929 Goes to Mohave Desert to continue recovery, returns, and again rambles west on freight trains.

1930   Publishes four poems in *Voices*.

1931–1932   Drifting, riding the rails in the west.

1932   Determined to finish school, again returns to Lincoln. Begins field work with Nebraska State Museum.

1933   B.A., University of Nebraska; continues field work in archeology with museum.

            Begins graduate school in anthropology, University of Pennsylvania; Frank Speck becomes mentor.

1935   A.M., University of Pennsylvania.

1937   Ph.D., University of Pennsylvania. Dissertation: "Three Indices of Quaternary Time and Their Bearing Upon Pre-History: A Critique."

1937–1944   Begins teaching career at University of Kansas department of sociology and anthropology.

1938   Marries Mabel Langdon, former curator of American art collections at University of Nebraska.

1941–1944   Works in war effort by teaching anatomy to premed reservists in Kansas.

1944–1947   Professor and head of department of sociology and anthropology, Oberlin College.

1947   Receives grant for research in East African humanoid sites; refuses grant, accepts post at University of Pennsylvania as chairman of department of anthropology.

1948   Loses hearing for six months, begins to write "the concealed essay, in which personal anecdote was allowed gently to bring under observation thoughts of a more purely scientific nature"—the genesis of his style for *The Immense Journey*.

1949   Vice-president, American Anthropological Association; declines invitation to be nominated for president the following year (1950).

1949–1952   President, American Institute of Human Paleontology.

1950   Frank Speck dies after long illness.
          Commences research on Darwinian precursors for *Darwin's Century*.

1951–1954   Helps American Philosophical Society acquire its massive collection of Darwiniana, now second-best collection in the world.

1957   *The Immense Journey*, first book, published by Random House.

1958   *Darwin's Century* wins Phi Beta Kappa prize for best book in science.

1959   Publishes controversial Blyth article in American Philosophical Society *Proceedings*.

1959–1961   Provost, University of Pennsylvania.

1960   *The Firmament of Time*; elected member of American Philosophical Society.

1961   University of Pennsylvania creates special interdisciplinary chair for him, later named Benjamin Franklin Professorship.

1961–1962   Fellowship, Center for Advanced Study in the Behavioral Sciences, Stanford, California.

1962–1964   Head, department of history and philosophy of science, University of Pennsylvania.

1963–1964   Guggenheim Fellowship for writing intellectual autobiography.

1969   *The Unexpected Universe*.

1971   *The Night Country*.

1972   *Notes of an Alchemist*, first volume of new poetry.

1975   *All the Strange Hours*, his autobiography.
          Cosmos: The Universe of Loren Eiseley, film based on Eiseley's books, opens at Reuben Space Theatre, San Diego.

1977   *Another Kind of Autumn*, third volume of poetry.
          Dies of cardiac arrest, July 9.

1978   *The Star Thrower* published posthumously.
          Dedication of Loren Eiseley Library and seminar, University of Pennsylvania Museum.

1979   *Darwin and the Mysterious Mr. X*, edited by Kenneth Heuer, published posthumously.

Preface

Not long ago, a friend of ours found himself perusing a new anthology of science fiction.[1] It was a well-conceived book, arranging the stories of a dozen authentic modern masters under various thematic headings. Roger Zelazny, Robert Heinlein, J. G. Ballard, Arthur C. Clarke, and Samuel Delany had all contributed to the volume. Each section of the book also included a theoretical article to give the reader a nonfiction perspective on the theme in question. To our friend's great surprise, the lead selection was by Loren Eiseley. Eiseley? The naturalist, anthropologist, and historian of science? The author of *The Immense Journey*, that superbly written book about evolution that had so captivated the college community in the early 1960s? Did Eiseley also work in science fiction?

Intrigued, our friend read the piece. Entitled "The Star Thrower" and placed under the heading "Evolution/ Identity," it appeared to be a short story, though a very odd one. The main character, a scientist, has made a solitary journey to a lonely coastline. Afflicted by a brutalizing emptiness of spirit, he pictures himself as a dead skull within which a glaring eye turns round like a beacon light. Wherever the revolving eye turns, it sees decay and desolation. Far up the beach from his hotel room, the scientist meets a man who is determinedly flinging live starfish back out over the pounding surf to save them from the shriveling sun. This rescue operation strikes the scientist as fantastically useless. Nature for him has become purely a scene of deathly struggle: "The star thrower is a man," he thinks, "and death is running more fleet than he along every seabeach in the world." He returns to his bare hotel room to resume his despairing meditation.

The tale's action now becomes mental—the thought streams and dream patterns of the scientist. In his black reverie, the ideas of Darwin and Freud pass in review. He sees these thinkers as the great disenchanters, revealers of the war in organic nature and within the human psyche. He reflects that the awesome powers released by modern science have been placed at the disposal of an ignoble race, for modern humans are disillusioned creatures who know themselves to be killers. Autobiographical material now appears. Down several roads of remembrance the scientist pursues his deaf mother. She appears to him in all her pain, coaxing him to view the world through her eyes and to love its failures (she is one). The scientist's vision gradually merges with hers; something cathartic happens. In the midst of this emptiness, a measure of pity and humility is delivered to him. The story closes with a magnificent scene: the narrator returns to the roaring beach to assist the star thrower— but not as a scientist. Now he is a sufferer, and thus he fully participates in this insane act of mercy. "From Darwin's tangled bank of unceasing struggle, selfishness, and death, had arisen, incomprehensibly, the thrower who loved not man, but life," he confesses.

"The Star Thrower" both delighted and perplexed

our friend. He read it through again, remarking its suggestiveness, haunting beauty, and compelling symbolism. The work bristled with ideas, but so profuse and varied was their array that he doubted that he could summarize them. Eiseley had avoided exposition and argument; the intellectual material of his piece had the concentrated, flowing quality of poetry. Form and content blended in a natural but wholly unusual way. Was this science fiction, speculative fiction, theory, intellectual autobiography, or all of these? Its chief artistic inspiration could be surrealism, but there were distinct traces of existentialism, imagism, and German romanticism. In any case, "The Star Thrower" was a masterpiece. Our friend mentally thanked the editors of the anthology and vowed to find out what else Loren Eiseley had been up to since *The Immense Journey*.

We suspect that our friend's experience is not unique. There must be thousands of readers who have chanced onto "The Mind as Nature," "Paw Marks and Buried Towns," "The Most Perfect Day in the World," "One Night's Dying" or "Big Eyes and Small Eyes"—exquisite pieces that have appeared in a bewildering assortment of periodicals and anthologies. Like "The Star Thrower," these essays blend narration and exposition in a marvelously complicated and effective way. In them all there is at least an echo of Eiseley's great theme: "Evolution/Identity," as the editors put it.

Does the present contain and recapitulate the evolutionary past? Are we not vitally linked to our extinct humanoid ancestors? Is there not an inner evolution of consciousness—an inner galaxy to explore? What meaning have the words "mercy" or "pity" in a Darwinian world? What mysteries and adventures await those researchers who labor patiently to make dead cities live again? How can wonder and enchantment be recovered by minds obsessed with finding explanations? Are memory and imagination defenses against the disordering potency of time?

These are Eiseley's questions, the generating tensions of all his art. Increasingly, these are the questions many sensitive souls are asking. This fact guarantees that Eiseley discoverers will multiply (all of Eiseley's books are presently in print), inevitably creating a demand for more and better Eiseley collections. The writing is too good, the ideas too rich and pertinent, to be left to the fortunate happenstance.

For the same reason, a secondary literature on Eiseley needs to develop. Fortunately, since Eiseley's death in 1977, a strong movement in that direction has surfaced. Articles, monographs, and dissertations assessing Eiseley's various achievements are beginning to appear. Our effort here, an expression of that movement, is the first book on Loren Eiseley. Aimed at the general reader, it provides a full introduction to Eiseley's writing. Beginning with biography, it proceeds to consider Eiseley's literary identity (he is principally an essayist), his work in the history of science, his key themes, his surrealistic ventures, and his achievement as an autobiographer. Throughout, we have constantly striven to reveal the beauty and richness of Eiseley's writing. We have given far more emphasis to his prose than to his poetry.

The book transcends its description of "introduction" in one crucial respect. We have distilled Eiseley's ideas into six perspectives or motifs. These constitute the Eiseleyan outlook—a delicate and powerful philosophic sensibility that emerges in all his writing. In a synoptic way, we present this distillation of Eiseley's thought at the end of Chapter 3. It then becomes the principle of organization for the remainder of the book.

List of Abbreviations

Loren Eiseley's works, frequently cited throughout this book, are indicated parenthetically by their abbreviations, listed below. The page numbers refer to the edition noted here, usually a readily available paperback volume.

AKA: *Another Kind of Autumn* (New York: Scribner's, 1977).

ASH: *All the Strange Hours: The Excavation of a Life* (New York: Scribner's, 1975).

DC: *Darwin's Century* (Garden City, N.Y.: Doubleday Anchor Books, 1961).

DM: *Darwin and the Mysterious Mr. X: New Light on the Evolutionists* (New York: E.P. Dutton, 1979).

FT: *The Firmament of Time* (New York: Atheneum, 1978).

IA: *The Innocent Assassins* (New York: Scribner's, 1973).

IJ: *The Immense Journey* (New York: Random House [Vintage Books], 1959).

IP: *The Invisible Pyramid* (New York: Scribner's, 1970).

MWS: *The Man Who Saw Through Time* (New York: Scribner's, 1973).

NA: *Notes of an Alchemist* (New York: Scribner's, 1972).

NC: *The Night Country* (New York: Scribner's, 1971).

ST: *The Star Thrower* (New York: Times Books, 1978).

UU: *The Unexpected Universe* (New York: Harcourt Brace Jovanovich [Harvest/HBJ Books], 1969).

Alchemist
of the Heart

"Are we quite sure who Loren Eiseley is?" This was Otto Friedrich's exasperated question as he reviewed *The Night Country* in 1971.[1] Friedrich simply could not reconcile the "solemnly institutional," archly academic Eiseley with the vulnerable insomniac who narrates that book's startling Gothic tales. Others have had trouble identifying Loren Eiseley. Critics and commentators have labeled him variously: social philosopher, a scientist's poet, literary anthropologist, philosophical naturalist, mystic, holistic environmentalist. None of these is inaccurate, yet neither are they neatly consistent.

Eiseley's self-identifications only complicate the matter: "drifter," "fugitive," "gambler," "changeling," "stranger," "freak." These words are evasions as much as answers. They betray Eiseley's fierce reluctance to play the identification game. In a characteristic gesture, Eiseley subtitled *The Night Country* "Reflections of a Bone-Hunting Man" but then withdrew this revealing phrase from the paperback edition issued a few months later. Shortly before Eiseley's death in 1977, E. Fred Carlisle wrote, "He has never quite fit the neat cages we have built to separate animals, people, and gods, the past from the present or scientists from poets, and he has always deliberately fled from such confinement."[2] In his autobiography Eiseley was more blunt: "I did not care for taxonomic definition, that was the truth of it."[3] Why Eiseley should have so resisted classification is partly evident from his biography.

Loren Corey Eiseley, descended from two generations of westward pioneers, was born September 3, 1907, in Lincoln, Nebraska. Economically and socially insecure, Eiseley's immediate family could provide him with only uneven and sporadic care. An actor and itinerant hardware salesman, Clyde Edwin Eiseley was not able to give his adoring son Loren the time the boy so desperately craved. Forty years difference in age and physical distance too often separated them. Clyde Eiseley's marriage to Loren's mother was his second. His beloved, deceased first wife was rarely mentioned during Loren's childhood. Fourteen years divided Loren from his half-brother, Leo, who influenced him little. The small impoverished family moved frequently within Nebraska—to Fremont when Loren was three, to Aurora seven years later, then back to Lincoln during his high-school years.

Loneliness thus plagued Eiseley's boyhood, a loneliness drastically intensified by his mother's handicap. Daisy Corey Eiseley had lapsed into total deafness in early girlhood. Beautiful and artistically gifted (her father in bad times would sell her paintings to saloons), she constantly "walked the precipice of mental breakdown" (UU, p. 86). Eiseley remembered most vividly her arbitrariness, her "harsh and jangling" voice, hysteria, stinginess. In *All the Strange Hours*, his powerful autobiography, Eiseley writes: "It comes to me now in retrospect that I never saw my mother cry; it was her gift to make others suffer instead" (p. 22). Lack of hearing rendered her paranoid. Suspicious of the few friends Loren made, she persisted in driving them away. The family lived on the edges of towns and Loren grew up in an unnatural silence. He felt most at home with animals and books. "In the quiet social isolation of his childhood, he kept intimate company with largely other than human beings," Ward Goodenough has reported. "He dealt with the contents of abandoned houses, of woods, fields and stream edges."[4]

By taking refuge in this way, Eiseley gained an intimate early knowledge of a remarkable region. His own ramblings, his family's mobility, his innate responsiveness to environments served to tie him psychologically

to the sunflower forests and salt-flat plains of eastern
Nebraska. Here remnants of Indian, pioneer, and prehistoric life were to be discovered. Ruts left by Conestoga
wagons bound for the Oregon country were still visible
on the prairie outside Aurora. A generation after Willa
Cather, Eiseley absorbed the same stimuli that awakened
Cather's great regional art. But Eiseley also knew the
dusts of the Depression; they imparted a special quality
to his regionalism. "No matter how far I travel," he wrote,
"it will be a fading memory on my tongue in the hour
of my death. It is the taste of one dust only, the dust of
a receding ice age" (ASH, p. 25).

Not all of Eiseley's early memories were painful or
desolate. He recalls a wonderful, rare moment of un-
animity between his parents when they decided to keep
him out of kindergarten, thus prolonging his freedom to
play and explore. During that year, Leo came home for
a brief visit. He brought with him the unabridged version
of *Robinson Crusoe* and read parts of it aloud to Loren.
After he left, the boy vowed to finish it himself. With
the help of an inadequate dictionary, he taught himself
to read and kept the vow. His father rewarded him with
a copy of a Jules Verne classic, and Eiseley's alliance with
books was permanently cemented.

There were other fond memories. In *The Night Country* Eiseley tells how he once escaped "the echoing loneliness of a house with no other children" by stowing away
on the back of a tea wagon. He had earlier found a small,
lovely toy wheel made of a gold-colored alloy. It became
"a sort of fetish," and his fascination with it transferred
to the tea wagon, with its bright golden-yellow wheels.
Finally an opportunity came, and the boy set off on a
great adventure through city streets and country roads.
"I jounced and bumped but my hold was secure," Eiseley
wrote. "Horseshoes rang and the whole bright world was

one glitter of revolving gold" (NC, p. 8). The autumn day exuded "the kind of eternal light which exists only in the minds of the very young." He wound up hiding in a hedge with hundreds of migrating brown birds, waiting out a storm. As he trudged soggily home, he had the half-delicious sensation that "I had been on the verge of a great adventure into another world that had eluded me" (NC, p. 10).

Eiseley discovered his interest in physical anthropology early. As a boy in Lincoln he frequently visited the university museum, fascinated especially by the skull collection. He modeled marble-sized clay heads from memory, and his grandmother baked them for him, shaking her head at these heretical "Darwinian" forms. An early interest in water ecosystems came to him via Eugene Smith's *The Home Aquarium*. Determined to build and stock a functioning aquarium in mid-winter, the young Eiseley nearly drowned in the thinly frozen pond while collecting his specimens.

As for his literary vocation, Eiseley tells of two seminal incidents. His love for the nature stories of Ernest Thompson Seton and Charles G. D. Roberts prompted him to confess in a high-school English class essay, "I want to be a nature writer" (ASH, p. 75). The second incident occurred during his freshman year in college. He was falsely accused of plagiarism in his first English assignment. "You didn't compose this; it is too well written," accused the teacher. The incident doused Eiseley's pleasure in the formal subject of English. He would not discover his gift for the literary essay for twenty years.

Eiseley enrolled at the University of Nebraska in 1925 but did not graduate until 1933. The exact chronology of this period is hard to establish. It certainly encompasses the most important and difficult events of his life—the Depression and Dust Bowl, his father's

death, his growing bitterness toward his mother, his bout
with tuberculosis, his drifting and dangerous days riding
the rails, the first real recognition of his writing ability,
and the first archeological field work.

In 1927, Nebraska's new literary magazine, *The Prairie Schooner*, included a short prose piece entitled "Autumn—A Memory," by Loren Eiseley. In it he meditates
on ruins, adopting the viewpoint of an ancient Aztec.
The style of *The Immense Journey* is clearly foreshadowed.
In 1928, Eiseley became one of the *Schooner*'s editors. In
the following year poems by classmate Mabel Langdon
appeared there. She and Eiseley later married.

But now a sadder, severer chapter begins. Eiseley,
like everyone else, saw his fortunes change because of
the Great Depression. During its first catastrophic year,
Eiseley's father died slowly and painfully of cancer. By
then, the youth had already dropped out of school, join-
ing the crowds of unemployed drifters who rode freights
across the country. A letter about his father's imminent
death reached him in San Francisco. Using the rails again,
he rushed home, nearly losing his life in a desperate fight
with a brakeman. Eiseley never forgave his mother for
her harsh question to the dying man about insurance.
After the funeral, Eiseley's aunt, terrified of contagious
disease, burned all his father's personal effects. Eiseley,
chancing on a pile of burning letters, noted a phrase about
himself, "the boy is a genius." The message gave him
the courage to continue.

Working insanely hard at a chicken hatchery while
he attended school part-time, Eiseley became very ill.
Tuberculosis was diagnosed. With the little money left
him by his father—his mother refused to contribute—
Eiseley traveled to Manitou Springs, Colorado, at the
foot of Pike's Peak, for a rest cure. Soon the money was
gone and Eiseley came back to Lincoln, still in extremely

poor health. This time a kindly university professor came to his rescue and arranged an easy job for him at the ranch of a wealthy woman in the Mohave Desert in California. His adventures there with Nelson Goodcrown, the chauffeur, and Mrs. Lockridge, the wealthy matron, he narrates wonderfully in "The Desert" chapter of *All the Strange Hours*—tales of pack rats and desert vastnesses and caring for Nelson during his drunken sojourn to Tijuana.

He returned to Nebraska the following October, desultorily began university extension courses, could not concentrate, and rambled west again on freight trains. A real drifter now, he almost perished several times in those desperate months and years. Time now becomes impossible to chart, as much of America was similarly adrift.

We gathered like descending birds in spite of all obstacles. Like birds, some of us died because we were old and we perished, unnoticed, of cold in the high Sierras or we slipped under the wheels of freights in moments of exhaustion. If found, what remained was buried in nameless graves along the track. Cheap liquor killed us; occasionally we died by the gun and so did the railroad detectives, pushing their luck too far with sullen unknown men in the night on swaying car tops. [ASH, p. 50]

Once, determined to cling to a fast freight and ride all the way back across Kansas, he miraculously awakened just as he was slipping toward certain death.

Finally he stopped running and returned to finish his degree, helped by a job as field worker in excavations for the Nebraska State Museum. His classmate and long-time friend C. Bertrand Schultz helped land him the assignment. Eiseley would later dedicate *The Innocent Assassins* to "The bone hunters of the old South Party, Morrill Expeditions 1931–1933, and to C. Bertrand Schultz, my comrade of those years." The experiences in western Nebraska's Badlands fossil beds gave him the direction he needed to choose graduate school in anthropology at the University of Pennsylvania. The job also provided Eiseley with a much-needed financial boost, and, most importantly, it solidified his unique aesthetic. As Bob Lancaster has written,

his experiences out there in the sandstone arroyos, the bat-infested caves, the sunflower fields, the prairie-dog towns, the mountain passes where cattle stood frozen in the snowdrifts, the remote places with undisturbed evidence of campfires built 10,000 years before by roaming hunters of forgotten tribes, influenced him profoundly. The vast solitude and timeless grandeur of that country would set the mood and suggest the themes for some of his best writing later on.[5]

In 1933, the westerner finally journeyed east, determined now to pursue his calling of "bone hunting." He quickly became a protege of department chairman Frank Speck, himself a pupil of Franz Boas, the dean of American anthropologists. Eiseley won Speck's respect early when he correctly identified some square-cut flints as not Indian but eighteenth-century gun flints. Still, graduate school in Philadelphia was lonely and forbidding, and he was often tempted to quit. "On my first day in Philadelphia," he once wrote, "I sought refuge on a tombstone in the heart of Woodland Cemetery, near the University. I had just come direct from months of fossil hunting in the Western Badlands, and the uproar of a great eastern city was almost unendurable."[6] Used to the dryness of the west, Eiseley could not adjust to the cold damp weather, and a severe ear infection in 1933 presaged more severe aural problems in later life.

His maternal uncle had helped send him to the University of Pennsylvania, and that faith and the blossoming friendship with Speck kept Eiseley working for the doctorate. His summers were spent on archeological expeditions at various sites in the American west. Working quickly, he finished the master's program in 1935 and the Ph.D. in 1937. His dissertation, "Three Indices of Quaternary Time and Their Bearing Upon American Pre-History: A Critique"[7] became the basis for much of his early research. In those very straitened times, the demand for anthropologists was pitifully low, and Eiseley was convinced he would have to seek other work. But a week before his degree was awarded he was offered a post as assistant professor of sociology and anthropology at the University of Kansas.

Eiseley endured those hectic first months as a college teacher—"the bitter soil of Kansas gritting in my teeth after each lecture."[8] He fought to keep abreast of the class and hold the attention of the football players in the back row. Gradually he discovered the value of illustrating his lectures by narrating adventures from his field work. In a 1974 interview, Eiseley speculated that this device unconsciously shaped his later literary style.[9] Thus the shy taciturn boy from the Dust Bowl was suddenly "talking for a living" and developing real showmanship. His father had made their household "echo with cadences of the drama and lost fragments of poetry,"[10] and Loren Eiseley relied on his example in these early years of teaching. In a fine chapter in his autobiography, Eiseley compared his thirty-year career as a lecturer to the life of Madeline, a "bowing" ginger cat he once knew. Having accidentally produced a fine curtsy, Madeline kept it up for the sake of the applause it evoked. Despite his success at "exhorting others from a platform," as he called it, Eiseley never felt completely at ease doing it. "For me," he wrote, "it has been a lifelong battle with anxiety" (ASH, p. 132).

In 1938, Eiseley married Mabel Langdon. They had become engaged before he left Nebraska, and she had

become curator of American art at the University of Nebraska.* War was beginning to cloud Europe, but not
until Pearl Harbor did Eiseley's students take it seriously.
Then, overnight, Lawrence, Kansas, changed utterly.
Eiseley, as a physical anthropologist with a background
in anatomy and biology, was shifted into teaching anatomy in the premedical program for reservists. Eiseley's
own intense desire to take a more active part in the war
effort was frustrated. Minor visual and hearing defects
were discovered, and affidavits concerning his mother's
mental condition may have played a role in the rejection.
He had hoped to work with provisional military governments of captured Pacific islands, applying his knowledge
of cultural anthropology. His motives were also financial.
His wife ailing and much of his salary going to support
his mother and aunt, Eiseley had to borrow to meet all
his bills. Within a year, however, he was offered a much
better position than the one he held at Kansas, as professor and head of the department of sociology and anthropology at Oberlin College.

The Kansas and Oberlin years were those of an
academic anthropologist. He published scholarly articles
and reviews in such journals as *The American Anthropologist* and was active in the American Anthropological
Association. Archeological field trips broadened his understanding of the tertiary and quaternary periods. Eiseley was establishing himself professionally in teaching,
research, and administration. A literary vocation seemed
to have passed him by; he published little poetry during

*To the end of his life, Eiseley remained extraordinarily
secretive about his marriage. His autobiographical writings reveal nothing about Mabel Langdon. By all accounts, Eiseley
drew immense strength from the relationship, which endured
for over forty years. It was perhaps the very success of the
marriage that made him protect it through silence.

this period and was no longer a contributing editor of *The Prairie Schooner*.

Then, in 1947, after he had received a grant for research in East Africa, he was called back to Pennsylvania to head the anthropology department he had left ten years before. Eiseley's task was to rebuild a badly demoralized unit. Frank Speck, the former chairman, had made a number of enemies, and the university had scheduled his department for oblivion. Emphasis was to be placed on the University Museum, which had long been at odds with Speck. After the museum's director committed suicide, however, a movement toward unity began. Froelich Rainey, the new museum director, accepted the post only on condition that the anthropology department be rejuvenated. Eiseley was sought with this goal in mind.

The critical nature of the situation forced Eiseley to forego research in Africa. Had he taken a leave then, he once said, "lurking forces would have sought to staff and commit the department to a course I deemed unwise" (ASH, p. 179). He sought to cement relations with the museum by involving curators and faculty on an equal basis in a common scientific enterprise. Extraordinarily capable people were hired (A. I. Hallowell, Ward Goodenough), and the department was gradually imbued with Eiseley's humanistic and interdisciplinary outlook. As a teacher, Eiseley was famous in these years for a graduate course entitled "Human Paleontology." His lectures, into which he put all his maturing ideas, drew large crowds— from which Eiseley would escape during the closing sentences of his lectures.

A year after the move to Philadelphia, in a dreary damp winter, Eiseley abruptly lost his hearing. Terrified he would become like his mother, Eiseley consulted a specialist, who diagnosed otitis media, infection of the middle ears and closed Eustachian tubes. For six months Eiseley received treatment, and gradually the hearing returned. But out of the frightening silence of that "ghost world," a different Eiseley emerged, one less worried about academic pigeonholes or the niceties of scholarly style. He began writing personal essays, trying to quench his fear of total deafness. Slowly he formulated what he later called "the concealed essay, in which personal anecdote was allowed gently to bring under observation thoughts of a more scientific nature" (ASH, p. 177). His first work in this vein, "The Fire Apes," appeared in *Harper's* and became the genesis of *The Immense Journey*.[11] His newfound form helped him assert his independence of academia. "I had lived so long in a winter silence that from then on I would do and think as I chose," he said. "I was fond of my great sprawling subject, but I had learned not to love anything official too fondly, even high office" (ASH, p. 178). Published in 1957 when Eiseley was 50 years old, *The Immense Journey* brought him a new audience and fame far beyond the scientific community. It was used as a college text, reprinted many times, and translated into more than ten languages.

Eiseley's nonscholarly writing continued, but in the early 1950s he found himself immersed in a major study of the history of evolutionary thought. Always interested in science's colorful past, Eiseley had slowly been building an admirable private collection of materials about the history of geology and biology. In connection with his research for what became *Darwin's Century* (1958), he helped the American Philosophical Society acquire its massive collection of Darwin materials.

While doing this bibliographic work, Eiseley made a surprising discovery. In 1959, he published a paper in which he argued that a version of the idea of natural

selection had been set forth by a forgotten English zoologist, Edward Blyth.[12] Darwin, Eiseley claimed, must
certainly have been much influenced by Blyth's articles
of the mid-1830s, which dealt with both natural and
sexual selection. But Darwin never credited Blyth, and
thus doomed this intriguing figure to obscurity. Eiseley's
theory provoked controversy at the time, and the issue
has been rekindled recently with the appearance of a
posthumous collection of Eiseley's Blyth-related articles
and their supporting documents. *Darwin and the Mysterious Mr. X* (1979), as it is called, clearly shows Eiseley's
emotional identification with Blyth. In his autobiography, Eiseley spoke of unearthing Blyth's whisper from
"the crumblings of the past" and expressed bitterness
about the cult of Darwin, which prevents acknowledgement of Blyth's achievement.

In 1959, Eiseley accepted an invitation to become
provost of the University of Pennsylvania. With the exception of some lectures delivered at the University of
Cincinnati and later issued in 1960 as *The Firmament of
Time*, his writing career ceased. For two years he floun-
dered in just the sort of detail work he had despised as
a department head. He later claimed that his only ad-
ministrative legacy of his provost years was an area of
the campus rebuilt to ensure pedestrian safety. Despite
an evident talent for academic leadership (on several occasions he was wooed by other institutions for their top
office), Eiseley surrendered his provostship in 1961. "The
restless turbulence that was to culminate in the student
violence of the sixties was just beginning to rap tentatively
and then ever more loudly on the door," he wrote (ASH,
p. 200). Eiseley foresaw larger troubles and knew that if
he remained in academic administration during great upheavals, his writing career would end.

After another university offered Eiseley an attractive research post, Pennsylvania created an interdisciplinary professorship free of committee work and departmental obligations for him. Thereafter, he could do what he did best, teach and write, and let his wide-ranging intellect work on whatever problems he settled upon.[13] Thus Eiseley gained the ponderous title of Benjamin Franklin Professor of Anthropology and the History of Science and Curator of Early Man at the University of Pennsylvania. Anticipating jealousies and accusations, Eiseley went on leave to Stanford "while the dust settled" (ASH, p. 202). When he returned to Pennsylvania, he almost embraced the anonymity and obscurity that began to surround him. He moved into an enormous office in the museum. With its ivy-shaded windows, Eiseley's superb book collection, his idiosyncratic assemblage of skulls, busts, archeological treasures, and paintings, this "cave" became a famous emblem of Eiseley's personality.

Of the decade of the 1960s, Eiseley wrote, "In one breath I suppose I could call it a ten-year ice age, in another the happiest time of my life, because in that great, gloomy half-circle office the little flames warmed and crackled about me" (ASH, p. 202). He read and wrote largely for his own plesaure. Gradually, he was becoming, observed John Medelman, "the academics' chaplain."[14] Technical studies gave way to philosophically expansive essays, beautifully fashioned short narratives, literary and historical studies. In 1962 he published *The Mind as Nature*, a reworking of his lectures for the John Dewey Society.[15] The thesis of the book echoes Eiseley's contentment with his new situation: "Sometimes the rare, the beautiful, can only emerge or survive in isolation. In a similar manner, some degree of withdrawal serves to nurture man's creative powers" (NC, p. 204). In 1963, a

series of Eiseley's addresses on Francis Bacon were released under the title *Francis Bacon and the Modern Dilemma*.[16] In 1964, he received a Guggenheim fellowship
to assist him in writing his own intellectual autobiography.

Although autobiographical references had enlivened
most of his earlier work, Eiseley found the Guggenheim
assignment almost too challenging. Ten more years would
pass before his "excavation of a life" could be completed.
Meanwhile, there were films to narrate, occasional courses
to teach, lectures to deliver, honorary degrees to receive,
fan mail to answer, and new chairmanship duties to carry
out. (Eiseley had founded a graduate program in the
history and philosophy of science; for two years he directed it.) His writing continued, and now it included
poetry too. But the overwhelming social cataclysms of
the sixties began to draw Eiseley out of his academic
shelter. Violent student protests and ideological mili-
tancy were abhorrent to him, and he spoke out. In a 1965
radio interview, for example, he accused students of ex-
pecting "Roman entertainment," submitting to mass hysteria, and destroying the esteem that professors had
rightfully earned through decades of study.[17]

Eiseley's embittered pronouncements were not the
statements of a reactionary. He regarded establishment
science as having betrayed a high calling. To the environmental crisis, which he had long foreseen, he re-
sponded with his own form of activism. He helped write
the Sierra Club's seminal volumes on the redwoods and
the Galapagos Islands.[18] These books launched the group's
campaign for an Earth Natural Park. Susan R. Schrepfer
sees Eiseley as the club's leading intellectual force during
this period. Eiseley's *The Unexpected Universe* (1969) and
The Invisible Pyramid (1970) contained the philosophic ba-

sis of an ecologic ethic. Thanks to these writings, says
Schrepfer, "To many Club leaders . . . , nature had rights
that should not be continually compromised for the benefit of man."[19]

In the early 1970s Eiseley's later poetry began to see
print. The first volume, *Notes of an Alchemist* (1972)
signaled a major departure from Eiseley's tightly controlled early verse. The new pieces moved in free forms
and tended to be lengthy. Most tended toward the
didactic and elegiac. The same was true for the other
two volumes, *The Innocent Assassins* (1973) and *Another
Kind of Autumn* (1977). For many readers, Eiseley seemed
to be operating in a curious space between poetry and
prose. Thematically, the poems celebrate nature's sovereign autonomy, foresee a new ice age, lament the
passage of primitive culture, compress vast time spans
into visual images, and summon timeless death. E. Fred
Carlisle observes that

> the poetry in these volumes reveals a solitary man: one who is
> sometimes lonely and melancholy, yet feels close to nature and
> to us—one who loves the world while he despairs of it—and
> one who doubts man's survival in the long scheme even while
> he recognizes man's great leap beyond nature.[20]

These words are also applicable to the person who
emerges in Eiseley's autobiography, *All the Strange Hours:
The Excavation of a Life* (1975). But whereas the late poetry
lacked a certain control and discipline, the autobiography
showed a master craftsman's touch. Critics were struck
both by the curious way Eiseley unfolded his tale and
by his ability to tell us so much and yet so little about
himself.* The work, going backward and forward in time,

---

*But some revealing concerns keep surfacing: a regret over

depends upon Proustian epiphanies of *mémoire involun-taire*, triggered by specific sense impressions. Finally he brings all the disparate strands together with the meta-phor of the outwash fan of a stream bed. That outwash fan, said Eiseley, is memory, "and it is from memory that we hesitantly try to reconstruct the nature of each individual torrent" (ASH, p. 249).

In *All the Strange Hours*, Eiseley says, "Toward the end, called variously writer, naturalist, scientist, I feel im-pelled to deny everything and hide what is left as best I may" (ASH, p. 248). But can a proper label not be found? Perhaps the best description of Eiseley would not be "naturalist," "scientist," or "writer," but rather "magi-cian," "shaman," or "alchemist"—terms he used for Speck, but that he also wanted to apply to himself. We are, he says in a poem, "alchemists of the heart" who

> . . . never solved a thing
> but lived lives close to where solutions were
> and did not want them,
>   preferred mystery.[21]

On July 11, 1977, Eiseley died in a Philadelphia hospital. Cancer of the pancreas was the cause of death, so perhaps he felt close to his father in those last days.

---

not having children and a bitterness about the academic rec-ognition he did not receive from his colleagues. The first he attributes to his early fear of the genetic carryover of his moth-er's paranoia and the "mad Shepards" in her family; by the time he understood how little he was at risk he had made his choice. "No children watch from the doorway as I write. Nor, if they crowded there, would I have a consistent narrative to bequeath them" (ASH, p. 228).

His motto could have been this sentence from G. K. Chesterton, one of his favorite writers, an epigram with which he headed one of the sections of his autobiography: "One must somehow find a way of loving the world without trusting it; somehow one must love the world without being worldly." Eiseley trusted not the world but individual beings in it, identifying beyond defini- tional borders with whatever creatures he came in contact with. That was the world he loved, as, like an alchemist, he transcended the borders that hedged him in—borders of time, of species, of profession, of class.

2

Eiseley's Medium: The Essay

What kind of writing did Loren Eiseley produce? The answer seems obvious enough: as we have noted, Eiseley wrote histories of science, technical papers in anthropology, popular articles with scientific themes, poetry, and autobiography. Unfortunately this categorization serves only as a rough preliminary guide, one whose shortcomings quickly appear. Because Darwin and evolutionary ideas dominate Eiseley's entire effort, almost all his writing could be described as "history of science" in some sense. As for separating out Eiseley's poetry, James Schwartz accurately observes that "Eiseley *is* a poet, of course; but most of his poetry, like Thoreau's, is found in his prose."[1] Nor will it do to isolate *All the Strange Hours* as Eiseley's sole exercise in autobiography. In most of what Eiseley wrote, he revealed some facet of his own experience and vision. The "concealed essay" was Eiseley's attempt to humanize scientific explanation with personal anecdote.

A common-sense approach to classifying Eiseley's work thus proves inadequate.[2] But is there a need for something better? Anyone familiar with Eiseley must answer yes. For if Eiseley is regarded as an historian of science to be measured against others in the field, then his overall contribution will seem slight. Place him in the company of other popularizing scientists, and he will appear as merely the author of many beautifully written expositions, some of which rise to literary heights. If one ranks him among poets, he will be judged as marginal and a little out of date. Viewed as a research scholar, he defended only a few scientifically significant hypotheses.

The result of dividing up Eiseley's writing according to his professional roles or disciplines is clear. Neither his huge popularity nor his literary reputation can thereby be explained. Eiseley has apparently made a major contribution—but to what tradition?

20

Preeminently and fundamentally, Loren Eiseley is an essayist. Anthropologists, ecologists, friends of natural history, students of the history of science, ministers, philosophers, English teachers—all may know a different side of Eiseley's work. But all of them encounter masterful experiments in the essay. Even when Eiseley composed in other forms, his essayistic tendency, which worked like a great literary magnet, drew his work into unfamiliar shapes. To grasp the nature of Eiseley's effort and achievement, then, one must know something of the essay's heritage and its fate in our century.

The names to be associated with Eiseley's are Heine, Lamb, Hunt, Hazlitt, Emerson, and Thoreau—masters of the familiar essay. Ultimately, of course, Eiseley's essays have their roots in the classical *essai* of Montaigne. For Montaigne, the *essai* is a written composition that tries, weighs (i.e., assays), or attempts an idea or thesis. It serves as a vehicle for exploration rather than demonstration; it precedes a final argument, not the argument itself. Nevertheless, it stands independently, with an underived literary value. The *essai*, says Montaigne, is personal, the opinion of the narrator alone, revealing his whole self, complete and naked.[3] The essayist, in this tradition, presents reflections on commonplace incidents, appealing lyrically to the reader's emotions and intellect. Francis Bacon, about whom Eiseley wrote much, called essays "dispersed Meditaciones," and found them an especially suitable means of presenting his religious ideas.

Along with the Gothic tale and the lyric poem, the personal essay was a favored literary vehicle of the great Romantics. Fond of impassioned prose and oratorical flourish, they produced highly eloquent essays that tended toward the ornate and elegant. Romantics like Rousseau, Emerson, and Thoreau demonstrated the personal essay's potential for communicating the responses of the solitary individual to nature. Thoreau's work uniquely combined the keen observations of a trained naturalist with the visionary reach of romanticism. Nourished by Thoreau's example, a many-sided American natural-history essay tradition emerged. At times sentimental, excessively aesthetic, and mawkishly spiritual, this out-of-doors literary convention has produced some masterpieces. John Burroughs, John Muir, Edwin Way Teale, Sally Carrighar, Aldo Leopold, Rachel Carson, Annie Dillard—these are only a few of the major shapers of this variant of the personal essay.

In all its forms and traditions, the essay suffered a serious decline that began in the late nineteenth century. As Mary Rucker has pointed out, the essay flourishes only when society is relatively homogeneous, "providing a sense of community to which the essayist [can] appeal whether he [is] castigating the town or reflecting upon old china."[4] It flourishes in a slow, agrarian social order. But rapid industrial development demolishes small communal structures, obliterates tradition, quickens the pace of life, and reduces the number of shared values. Readers demand information, conclusions, plans of action, ideology. The *article* emerges as the dominant item in the periodical press. William Dean Howells noted the shift as early as 1902, and a writer in the *Saturday Review* in 1932 summarized the public's new attitude as "too impatient of the speculative, and too avid of accomplishment to tolerate the ruminative discursiveness of the easy chair philosopher."[5]

Despite its seemingly outmoded character, the essay has enjoyed the favor of such modern luminaries as G. K. Chesterton, George Orwell, Edward Weeks, and Joseph Wood Krutch. Significantly, all of these writers are hostile to industrial civilization and call for some sort of agricultural renewal. Krutch argues the need for the essay in an age obsessed with fragmented images of the human. The essay, he believes, treats human life familiarly and intimately; it refuses to reduce a human being to "the mechanical sum of the Economic man, the I.Q. man, and the other partial men with whom the various partial sciences deal."[6] Creative literature deals with the whole, and the personal essay is a form that can achieve this synthesis quickly and easily, claims Krutch.

As we have seen, Eiseley sensed very early his affinities with the natural-history essayists, especially Ernest Thompson Seton. Later, Chesterton came to serve as his model of essayistic style. It was not until after he evolved his "concealed essay" form that Eiseley discovered the compelling greatness of Thoreau and Emerson. He then made a careful study of both writers, producing fine literary-critical pieces about them.[7] Thoreau's elegant yet intimate style clearly had a marked influence on Eiseley's later work. Eiseley shared the discomfort that modern essayists have felt with urban, mechanized mass society. Indeed, he confessed his nostalgia for the small-town, midwestern America of his boyhood. Alien to him was the narrowly argumentative, positivistic, unadventurous modern temper.

"The Last Neanderthal," from *The Unexpected Universe*, shows something of Eiseley's unique way of adapting the personal essay tradition. As it imparts several important scientific ideas, the work anchors itself in Eiseley's innermost history and speculative life. Ostensibly, Eiseley's topic is "the sheer organizing power of animal and plant metabolism" (UU, p. 218). Cellular oxidation, the burning of stored chemical energy, produces higher and more concentrated energy forms. Those organisms that evolve more efficient mechanisms for hoarding, storing, and transfering energy survive and multiply. The organic world thus seems to contradict the second law of thermodynamics, which predicts that all systems run down to their least organized state. Eiseley does not hold his scientific subject matter at safe distance, however. In the essay, he entangles it in an intricate web of meditations and narratives so that the reader experiences the theories. In the end, we find that the second law is merely one more way of speaking about time, remembrance, estrangement from nature, and self-transcendence.

The essay is structured around three vivid memories that are triggered by a fourth. Eiseley recalls walking a deserted beach in Curaçao. He finds a dead dog wrapped in burlap, "obviously buried at sea and drifted in by the waves" (UU, p. 214). The simple thought that the creature once had lived strikes him forcefully. "Scenes on the living sea that would never in all eternity recur again had streamed through the sockets of those vanished eyes" (p. 215), he realizes. The equatorial sun is oppressive, and Eiseley takes shelter beneath a manzanillo tree. Its poison apples remind him of something. But the glare, the hummingbirds, and the darting lizards distract and confuse him.

Unbidden, a scene passes before his inner eye. It is 1923 in Lincoln, Nebraska. An absurdly heaped junk wagon crosses the intersection between R and Fourteenth streets. He is watching from a window one block away, "absorbed as only a sixteen-year-old may sometimes be with the sudden discovery of time" (p. 217).

Forty-five years later the horse and wagon still move through the intersection. "I was not wrong about the powers latent in the brain," reflects Eiseley. "The scene was still in progress" (p. 217). A scent of burning autumn leaves lingers about the memory; another experience has been evoked—of a plum tree thicket on an exquisite fall day. But now Eiseley is transported into a reflection about combustion—how the junk man on R Street is prevented from departing by the furious burning of oxygen in Eiseley's own brain. The junk man "is held enchanted" in cerebral neurons, which are themselves the basis of a new form of evolution.

Without explaining this intriguing idea, the essay shifts to another incident. For two months he and his companions have been digging American rhinoceros bones in the west. The site is a hapless, windblown farm with a sod house. A stocky, barefoot woman of twenty comes regularly to the archeologists' camp to sell provisions. One evening, as she approaches through shadows and firelight, Eiseley understands that the woman is a living fossil—a true Neanderthal:

Her head, thrust a little forward against the light, was massive-boned. Along the eye orbits at the edge of the frontal bone I could see outlined in the flames an armored protruberance that, particularly in women, had vanished before the close of the Wümerian ice. She swung her head almost like a great muzzle beneath its curls, and I was struck by the low bun-shaped breadth at the back. [UU, p. 222]

Lost in time, the woman seems to Eiseley the product of "a chance assemblage of archaic genes" still resident in the race (p. 228). Her gentle, shy, unreflective presence makes him intensely aware of both evolutionary time and cultural difference.

Later she asks him, "Do you have a home?" not realizing the irony of the question. A vivid symbol of humanity's vast evolutionary journey away from original nature, the woman does not herself comprehend that she speaks to Eiseley across one hundred thousand years. Both of them are homeless, but he more so, because he inherits the results of cultural evolution. In the fertile brain of modern man, a new sort of hoarding and concentrating is at work. A second nature compounded of scientific knowledge and technical proficiency allows humanity to threaten itself with total destruction. "A mathematical formula traveling weakly along the rivers of the neopallium may serve to wreck the planet," he observes. "It is a kind of metabolic energy never envisioned by the lichen attacking a rock face or dreamed of in the flickering shadows of a cave fire" (p. 230).

Thus *Homo sapiens*, the energy devourer, is embarked on a perilous career. Eiseley comprehends this all too vividly as he bids "the last Neanderthal" good-bye at the summer's end. Our "strange metabolism" has drawn us far away from the world we call natural; with brains stuffed with scientific knowledge, we now confront that world as alien, something to be manipulated. But, contends Eiseley, we cannot forsake our origins entirely. Although nature has produced consciousness and intelligence, at the bottom of things the oxidizing cell sustains; its "surreptitious burning to a purpose" makes its final claim (UU, p. 226).

This is the burden of the essay's final vignette. Eiseley, now grown old, visits the wild plum thicket he had remembered on the beach. Still puzzled by "this strange hoarding and burning at the heart of life," he wonders if he himself is anything more than "a sophisticated fire that has acquired an ability to regulate its rate of combustion and to hoard its fuel in order to see and walk" (p. 231). Smoke from the autumn fields penetrates his mind, the beauty of the plums assails him, and he lies back in the leaves. He thinks of the junk man needing release and of the "heavy-headed dreaming girl drawing a circle in the dust" (p. 232). His essential oneness with the smoke, fire, and tree becomes as plain as the fact that he is now burning out.

I wanted to drop them at last, these carefully hoarded memories. I wanted to strew them like the blue plums in some gesture of love toward the universe all outward on a mat of leaves. Rich, rich and not to be hoarded, only to be laid down for someone, anyone, no longer to be carried and remembered in pain like the delicate paw lying forever on the beach at Curaçao. [p. 232]

He experiences lightness, a lifting of the weight of the stored energy in memory, a cleansing of his spirit.

The essay closes with Eiseley limping off down the ravine, the bitter taste of plum in his mouth. He fingers a small flint blade he has carried about for years. It came from near the last Neanderthal's sod house, and by it Eiseley is linked to a world one hundred thousand years in the past. An emblem of technological mastery, it also recalls a time when humanity and nature were in better balance. The secret, says Eiseley, is to travel as much as possible in the natural world, or at least to know when one has evolved too far from it.

In "The Last Neanderthal," as in Montaigne's works, Eiseley's reader comes to identify with the hero of the action: the essayist himself. Argument and demonstration rarely surface, although a point—or, better, a moral— is developed. Scientific knowledge undergirds the essay, but the knowing scientist with his personal quest remains central. Eiseley writes for people who have time, who speculate, who are prepared to be disturbed. He builds complicated literary structures that bear many rereadings. To place the works in any other category than essay (the publisher of *The Unexpected Universe* called the book "nature writing") is to consign them to obscurity.

Eiseley produced some seventy-five essay-length pieces. The major themes developed in these writings will be

treated in subsequent chapters. For now, we must stress
that some of Eiseley's efforts fall outside the category of
the personal essay. Besides poetry and autobiography,
Eiseley explored four other literary forms: the journalistic
article, the scholarly treatise or paper, the short story,
and the sermon. What is striking about these, however,
is the way Eiseley's penchant for the personal essay shapes
their execution. This tendency is also apparent in Eiseley's poetry, his autobiography, and even his one big
book on evolution, *Darwin's Century*. At the same time,
Eiseley's work in these other genres greatly influenced
his approach to the essay per se. A rapid scan of these
other forms will thus prove useful.

Eiseley's articles appeared in such periodicals as *Hol-
iday*, *Scientific American*, the *Saturday Evening Post*, and
Life. Fine examples of scientific journalism, they marshall
a great many facts but sustain interest by placing them
in a suspenseful order. Eiseley's own inner dramas are
not revealed, but he exercises fully his ability to discover
spectacle and limn the picturesque. (W. H. Auden once
perceptively compared Eiseley to John Ruskin.[8]) "Easter:
The Isle of Faces" (ST) and "How Flowers Changed the
World" (IJ) epitomize this kind of journalism. Eiseley
closes the former article with this typical flight of rhetoric: "No tears are marked upon the faces, and when at
last the waves close over them in the red light of some
later sun than ours, the secret of mankind, if indeed man
has a secret, will go with them, and all will be upon that
waste as it has been before" (ST, p. 105). Eiseley also
wrote a few polemical articles, usually focusing on environmental problems. "The World Eaters," (IP) which
warned of uncontrolled population growth, is one such
effort.

The articles collected in *Darwin and the Mysterious
Mr. X* are Eiseley's most formidable scholarly papers.

Despite their orthodox and respectable execution, they reveal his artistic temper. As Kenneth Heuer has pointed out, in the central paper of the book Eiseley arranges his material to create the atmosphere of a detective story. Indeed, Eiseley first thought of presenting his discovery in the form of detective fiction. He even began a man-uscript but later laid it aside; Heuer appropriated its title for this posthumous work.[9] Some of Eiseley's finest per-sonal essays ("The Innocent Fox" [UU] and "The Star Thrower" [UU and ST], for example) are interwoven with brief mystery tales.

That Eiseley wrote pure fiction is not well known. The works are anthologized with his essays, and because the essays are often framed and infused with narrative, these short stories can be mistaken for them. "The Dance of the Frogs" (ST), "The Fifth Planet" (ST), "The Relic Men" (NC), "Barbed Wire and Brown Skulls" (NC), and "The Places Below" (NC) are key specimens.[10] All have the characteristics of the first-person tall tale, owing much to the legacy of Twain, Bierce, and Poe. They usually relate a story first told to the narrator by someone else. Settings are carefully drawn, suspense maximized, rhe-torical signs carefully placed. The narrator is the one who doubts the fantastical, horrific, and unusual events of the story but is finally drawn into the scene, per-suaded, and thus tries to persuade the reader.

Because Eiseley's essays draw so heavily on his fic-tionalizing talents, we should briefly linger over his finest tall tale, "The Dance of the Frogs" (ST). Eiseley's fond-ness for the Gothic could not be more evident. The nar-rator, presumably an anthropologist, "had long been a student of the strange melange of superstition and wood-land wisdom that makes up the religious life of the nature peoples" (ST, p. 106). He tells of a reclusive, morose old zoologist, Albert Dreyer, who has "journeyed farther

into the Country of Terror" than anyone else (p. 106).
Dreyer excitedly hears the narrator's scholarly lecture on
the religious beliefs of the Naskopi. In their rites, these
Labrador Indians communicate with "game lords," giant
versions of hunted animals—enormous archetypes that
both lead and empower animate nature.

After the lecture, the evening grown very late, Dreyer
hesitantly explains his excitement to his fellow scientist.
His gestures cause the narrator to notice once again the
black glove protecting Dreyer's hand. Years ago Dreyer
had had a secluded laboratory near the Schuylkill River.
After experimenting with small amphibia, he would often
take long midnight walks on a lighted but unused street.
One warm spring night, a great swarm of amphibious
life came forth from the surrounding marshes. Out of the
wet meadows emerged countless toads and frogs to hop
down the deserted road to the river. There, mating and
laying eggs, they fulfilled their impulse to unite with the
elemental water. On his midnight walk, Dreyer is be-
mused by the pageant and then drawn into it.

"I simply began to skip, to skip gaily, and enjoy the
great bobbing shadow I created as I passed onward with
that great leaping host all headed for the river," he confesses (ST, p. 112). But the pace accelerates, and, a spring
madness welling up in him, Dreyer loses himself in the
pell-mell energy of it all. His ecstasy tinged with fear,
he senses an additional presence, a "great, leaping gro-
tesquerie," shocking in size. Terrified, he dances on
madly. "You dare not look, because, beside the shadows,
there now comes to your ears the loose-limbed slap of
giant batrachian [amphibious] feet..." (p. 113). The archaic, elemental, insane dance presses on, carrying "the
mighty ecstasies of a thousand springs" (p. 114). The
zoologist senses his soul departing, his physical shape
modifying, his will to be human disappearing. At the

moment before he would have plunged off the dock, he summons a shout, appealing to the Christian deity under a cross-shaped shadow. He is freed. The crashing night is quiet, the game lords have departed. Dreyer's story is over. The narrator sits in confused silence, watching Dreyer sip a drink. Then Dreyer holds up his black hand and deliberately "pinches off" the glove.

A man should not do that to another man without warning, but I suppose he felt I demanded some proof. I turned my eyes away. One does not like a webbed batrachian hand on a human being. [p. 115]

Besides articles, treatises, and short fictions, Eiseley also produced what can only be called sermons. He claimed to have had little exposure to organized religion as a youth and in adulthood steered clear of formal observances. Yet midwestern Protestant oratorical traditions influenced him decisively. Some of his essays are almost purely homiletic exercises. They meditate on the main text (for example, a passage from Bacon or Darwin) and employ parable, anecdote, memorable epigram, rhetorical flourish, and moral exhortation. These devices appear in such abundance that the term "lecture" fails to describe the effect of these pieces.

"How Human is Man," from *The Firmament of Time*, reveals Eiseley's sermonizing inclination particularly well. Alarmed by our preoccupation with machines and manipulable processes, Eiseley calls for a renewal of inwardness. Deterministic and relativistic ideas have eroded the ethic of personal responsibility, he insists. "Group selfishness," especially evident in labor unions, fractures the social order. The claims of the individual soul are drowned out by an electronic, commercial roar. Like all sermonizers, Eiseley illustrates his views with personal anecdotes rather than supporting them with evidence. To close the piece, he does not summarize his conclusions but relates a little story. The physical anthropologist John Buettner-Jansch caustically described this essay as "a series of moral parables on a somewhat higher level than those found in the repertory of a fundamentalist preacher."[11] Presumably, Eiseley's other sermons—"The Chresmologue" (NC), "Man in the Autumn Light" (IP), "The Inner Galaxy" (UU)—would have provoked an even more hostile response. They are decidedly "unscientific."[12]

How Eiseley's essayistic bent manifested itself in his autobiography will be touched upon in Chapter 10. As for Eiseley's later poetry, it can almost be described as essayistic free verse. Except for its typography, it is nearly indistinguishable from his more lyrical prose. Thus, "Knossos" (AKA) is almost an article on the vanished Cretans, and "Desperate I Walked" (IA) is a polemic against pollution. "The Rope" (NA) and "The Maya" (AKA) are speculative, familiar essays; "The Figure in the Stone" (NA) is a short story, including dialogue, plot, and characters. "No Place for Boy or Badger" (AKA) is a sermon, as is "Why Does the Cold So Haunt Us" (AKA). The rhetorical techniques of the various prose forms are all in use in this poetry, though far greater use is made of analogy. So apparent is the essayistic character of this verse that one is tempted to see it as preliminary notes for actual prose pieces.

3

The Message of
Darwin's Century

That Loren Eiseley was deeply preoccupied with time is evident to even the most superficial reader of his works. Time and eternity, permanence and change, memory and oblivion, mythical and real time, relative and absolute time—these dichotomies dominate Eiseley's thought. In *The Night Country* he wrote, "My sense of time is so heightened that I can feel frost at work in stones, the first creeping advance of grass in a deserted street" (NC, p. 158). His obsession with time is more than a product of his training as an anthropologist and paleontologist. Something in his character made him return continually to this subject. A fossil hunter from youth, Eiseley found that his mind had become "imprinted by the visible evidence of time and change of enormous magnitude. To me time was never a textbook abstraction" (IA, p. 11).

As a high-school student, Eiseley eagerly read Jack London's *Before Adam* and Stanley Waterloo's *Story of Ab*, works that popularized evolutionary concepts. Eiseley's early poetry often meditates on endings, passings, and the eternal return of ancient and alien patterns. As early as "Dusk Interval" (1935), he sounds a theme that later emerges as a faint descant to all his lyrical writing: the coming of another ice age, when the tramp of mammoths "will shudder/The last man from his bed" (ST, p. 163).

But if early established elements in Eiseley's personality directed him toward anthropology, anthropology in turn decisively affected the way in which Eiseley thought about time and change. A social science, anthropology aims to discover models of explanation for the behavior of human groups. It pursues this goal by studying human origins and development, the major physical differences within the human family, the way races and cultures are distributed, and the social function of folkways and institutions. American anthropology, which developed out of natural history and native Amer-

34

ican ethnography, now embraces four subdisciplines: cultural, physical, archeological, and linguistic.* What binds
these specializations is their common concern for broad
developmental patterns in human social life, physical
structure, and language. Thus, evolution is the central
unifying idea of this vast science.[1]

By the early 1950s, Eiseley had already offered
courses in the history of evolutionary thought and was
clearly building a scholarly expertise in this area. This
development was hastened by a request from Doubleday
for a major book on Darwin's epoch. Not knowing quite
what would be involved, Eiseley accepted. There followed years of painstaking research in England and the
United States, years in which Eiseley amassed too much
material and made too many discoveries to be treated in
the single volume he had promised. His characteristic
sympathy for lost and forgotten things caused him to
study carefully those precursors of Darwin who had erred,
as well as those who had contributed to the discovery of
natural selection. "The history of science," he found, "is
as full of abandoned sink holes as a cavern. Theories
emerge, have their moment, and vanish or, on the other
hand, are slowly transformed into greater syntheses"
(ASH, pp. 185–186). Charmed by obscure evolutionary
thinkers, pulled by "the lure of documents," and driven

*Eiseley's unusual combination of physical anthropology,
paleontology (the study of the fossil record left by ancient plants
and animals), and American Indian ethnology seemed almost
designed to confront him with technical evolutionary issues in
the most intense way possible. His field work with the Nebraska Museum, his work with Speck on fossil dating, his experience as an amateur naturalist, his research on fire drives
and plant extinction all directed Eiseley's thought along those
avenues of anthropology where analysis of evolutionary notions
is most thorough going.

to personal reflection on the meaning of evolution, Eiseley produced no manuscript.

What brought *Darwin's Century* into being was a
characteristically Darwinian reality: competition. The
centennial of the publication of *The Origin of Species* (1859)
approached, and Eiseley knew that other scholars were
working to complete books dealing with Darwin and his
era. Under this stimulus, Eiseley "wrote till my eyes wept
from stress, . . . slept when tired without reference to day
or night, and arose and wrote again" (ASH, p. 185). And
he won. *Darwin's Century* appeared almost a year ahead
of John C. Greene's *The Death of Adam* and Gertrude
Himmelfarb's *Darwin and the Darwinian Revolution*. Eiseley's momentum carried him further. With the subsequent issuance of the Blyth articles and *The Firmament of
Time* (1960), Eiseley established himself not only as a
premier historian of science but also as a philosopher-
poet of evolution.

His long labors on evolution and the men who discovered it had a decisive impact on Eiseley's life and
career.* He emerged from the scholarly ordeal with new
intellectual heroes: James Hutton, Edward Blyth, Charles
Lyell, and A. R. Wallace. He found himself possessed
of a cause—to champion several forerunners of Darwin
whose contributions to evolutionary ideas had been ob-
scured or unrecognized. More important, by writing about
the technical and philosophical issues which Darwin had

---

*In *The Invisible Pyramid*, Eiseley wrote, "I was fifty years
old when my youth ended" (IP, p. 137). He referred to a
powerful experience of mistaking someone for his beloved teacher
and confidant, Frank Speck. Eiseley saw the experience as an
epiphany, a completion, a summons to take up his proper mission. Significantly, the incident occurred in the autumn of 1957,
just before the completion of *Darwin's Century*.

raised Eiseley deepened his understanding of the fullness of the Darwinian revolution. The research for *Darwin's Century* not only provided Eiseley's imagination with rich new subject matter; the work also brought focus, clarity, and unity to some of his most fundamental ideas. In the perceptive words of E. Fred Carlisle, Eiseley had "interiorized" the theory of evolution "so that it functions as a major structure for perceiving and comprehending experience. He dwells in it, and through it makes contact with reality."[2]

The major themes of Eiseley's later writing are all vividly present in *Darwin's Century*, especially its final chapters. In what Eiseley wrote in the succeeding two decades, he essentially elaborated and developed the synthesis he achieved in the late 1950s. *The Immense Journey* is also a product of this period; indeed, some chapters of the two books are interchangeable. In view of the great importance of *Darwin's Century* to Eiseley's literary career, some key features of the book deserve scrutiny here. There is another reason to pause over this work: for Eiseley, evolution was not merely a plausible hypothesis; it was a sensibility, a specific way of feeling and seeing. To appreciate the nature of that sensibility, he believed, one must understand how it grew in the minds not only of the Darwinians but also of their forebears. After surveying the major historical stages that Eiseley defines, we will present an overview of the major literary themes he derived from this scholarly effort.

As an historian of scientific ideas, Eiseley's achievements are many. But for the lay reader none is more noteworthy than Eiseley's grasp of the enormous difficulties the evolutionists overcame. Charles Darwin and the Reverend John Ray, author of *The Wisdom of God Manifested in the Works of the Creation* (1691), are separated by less than a century and a half, but these two English naturalists inhabit utterly different universes of thought. How the distance between these universes was traversed is a story Eiseley told with dramatic power and scientific clarity. He resisted the temptation to see pre-Darwinian concep- tual schemes such as Ray's as unfortunate hindrances to scientific advance. Rather, Eiseley understood the dia- lectical character of the intellectual process leading up to Darwin, a process in which erroneous theories and syntheses were the necessary preconditions to more ad- equate explanatory models.

Eiseley once asserted that four fundamental per- spectives had to be articulated, clarified, and fully com- prehended in order for Darwin's breakthrough to be possible. First, the great antiquity of the planet had to be grasped, for without this, the possibility of new life forms developing very gradually from minute variations does not exist. Second, it was necessary to establish "that there had been a true geological succession of forms on the planet." The plants and animals of the present had to be seen as descendants of much earlier, very different inhabitants of a continuously changing terrestrial envi- ronment. Third, the amount of individual variation in the living world and its possible significance in the cre- ation of change had to be understood. If evolution pro- ceeds through the preservation of characteristics that differentiate an individual from its species type, the de- gree and frequency of differentiation must be fully ap- preciated. Finally, the notion of a perpetually balanced world machine had to give way to a conception of the organic world as not being in equilibrium at all. Evolution would be possible, in Eiseley's words, only in a world "whose creations made and transformed themselves throughout eternity"—whose inner law is a dialectical and disharmonious readjustment of forces (FT, pp. 70–71).

What made the establishment of these four perspectives so difficult a task? Eiseley's general answer would be shared by most historians of Western thought: their formation requires "the transformation of a static conception of nature into a dynamic one" (DC, p. 6). Each presupposes, in Eiseley's words, "a universe not made but being made continuously" (DC, p. 9). Although the beginning of the eighteenth century witnessed the discussion of disturbing new biological and geological ideas, Europeans generally remained intellectually faithful to nonevolutionary views: the inerrancy of the Bible and its account of creation, the Christian conception of time, and the notion of a fixed scale or great chain of being. Each of these views reinforced the common-sense feeling that the earth and its life forms are given ready made from the hand of the Creator for the fulfillment of a preordained plan. And yet, as Eiseley shows, these perspectives also had an ironic role to play in stimulating the lines of evolutionary thought to which they are so opposed.

Christian Natural Philosophy:
The Attractions of Changeless Order

Read literally, Genesis presents a teleological, static picture of the biosphere. The world's flora and fauna are made by God for human use; the creation of humanity completes a good system, a creation whose smallest part reveals the divine intention and whose myriad gradations and forms are both caused and governed by the bountiful God. Specific geological facts are either the work of God's

direct artifice "in the beginning" or else the effect of such
major postcreation cataclysms as the Flood. Since its formation the organic world has changed little, for there has
not been time for major transformations to occur. (Bishop
James Ussher's famous date of 4004 B.C. for the creation
was only one of many such measures of time's essential
brevity.) Fixity, not change, dominates the biblical account. Beasts and birds are made "according to their
kind"; Adam names all living creatures, establishing their
role and function as servants of humanity. Despite the
human fall from grace, "the Works created by God at
first, [are] by Him conserved to this Day in the same
State and Condition in which they were first made," said
John Ray.[3] This must be so, because these works are
ordained to a higher purpose: to be the scenery and setting for time's central fact—God's final redemption of
humanity from the ravages of time itself.

For centuries, this scriptural viewpoint had been
buttressed by a classical idea that enjoyed great popularity among Christian intellectuals: the *scala naturae* or
great chain of being. Nature exhibits a series of ascending
stairs or levels, on which distinctive material and organic
forms are distributed. As Eiseley summarizes the notion,
"the Scale of Nature runs from minerals by insensible
degrees upward through the lower forms of life to man,
and beyond to purely spiritual existences like the angels"
(DC, p. 7). The concept thus blends physical with moral
significance. Higher is better as well as more complex.
Creatures lower on the scale resemble in their relative
grossness and simplicity the reign of the purely material.
Toward the top, elegance and the capacity for inner reflection dominate. For Aristotle, this hierarchical order
in nature reflected the human soul, in which the material
elements were naturally subordinated to the intellectual
and spiritual.

The great chain of being did not suggest an evolutionary relationship among the species. Its appeals were aesthetic and theological. It assumed that each species was perfect, created especially for its place in this well-proportioned scheme, unchangeable and distinctively useful to man. "Thus," writes Eiseley, "the resemblances between living things are not the result of descent with modification but rather are the product of the uniformity and continuity of the divine act" (DC, p. 8). In this view, newly discovered species are regarded as "missing links"—but not in the modern sense, which implies organic relatedness. The task of the reverent naturalist was to place his discovery in its divinely appointed box. As Eiseley points out, eighteenth-century scholars recognized that the ape stood next to the human on the scale of nature. They were not appalled by this, because they knew that the chain separated the species as much as it linked them.

What this Christian natural philosophy especially could not contemplate was the idea of species extinction. Nor could it accept time as vast and essentially endless. Extinction implies divine error, a break in the chain. The development of new species was equally unthinkable. So, affirmed John Ray, "since the first creation there have been no species of animals or vegetables lost, no new ones produced" (DC, p. 64). The notion of infinite time is un-Biblical; more frightening, however, is its implication that if time is boundless, the features of the earth might have emerged through the slow action of impersonal, mechanical forces rather than the loving, direct activity of God. If eons of time and huge populations of plants and animals did precede the present moment, surely so significant a fact would have been disclosed by God in His scriptural revelation.

The Challenge of Evidence and Uniformitarian Ideas

By the middle of the eighteenth century, a torrent of new
ideas and facts had emerged to challenge the precarious
synthesis of John Ray and other like-minded Christian
scientists. The physics of Galileo and Newton had created a new respect for mechanistic explanations and a
consciousness of the rule of mathematically based law
over all matter and motion. The telescope revealed an
immense universe, pockmarked planetary bodies, the
changeable aspect of the sun, and a galaxy in motion.
Whereas Aristotle had regarded sun and stars as eternal,
perfect, and divine, scores of thinkers now began to speculate on the origin and development of planetary systems.
"The timeless Empyrean heaven was now seen to be,
like the corrupt world itself, a place of endless change,
of waxing and waning worlds," writes Eiseley of this
period. And although the fact awaited geological demonstration, "the new astronomy with its vast extent of
space implied another order of time than man had here-
tofore known" (DC, p. 30).

The fossil record, which had been limited when John
Ray undertook to explain it, came dramatically into view.
Simultaneously, on Siberian and North American frontiers, pieces of a strange and massive elephant species
were being discovered. "There were now whispers," says
Eiseley, "that some of that buried life was no longer
present among the living" (DC, p. 36). The microscope
was increasingly being used to study reproductive cells
and the development phases of embryos. Data accumu-
lated that called into question the older "homunculus" or
preformation theory, which was intimately linked to the
idea of special creation. Eiseley argues that once it was

shown clearly that all organisms develop by degrees from a less differentiated substance, one could "accept with greater equanimity the conception that a species itself might come into existence by some more extended process of phylogenetic change" (DC, p. 37). In France, Deism increasingly challenged biblical authority and glorified nature as the true medium of divine revelation. In England, aristocrats and gentry became passionately interested in improving domesticated plant and animal species, thus acquiring an interest in the nature and causes of individual variation within a species.

Eiseley sees the Frenchman Benoit de Maillet (1656–1738) as a key indicator of this great intellectual change. A traveler, bureaucrat, and amateur naturalist, Maillet discarded Noah's flood as an explanation of the earth's features. His system, observes Eiseley, "is essentially uniformitarian, that is dependent upon the known and still operating forces of nature" (DC, p. 33). Maillet hypothesized that the continents had been shaped by a great primitive sea that once engulfed the planet. This sea, which Maillet thought was subsiding, engendered the first organic life, from which all terrestrial forms were derived. The dissipation of water will continue. "Eventually, the earth will be desiccated and itself become a sun, or escape, by fortune, to become part of another solar system" (DC, p. 35). Maillet's ideas, stresses Eiseley, rely on vast vistas of time, mechanical explanation, close observation, and the clockmaker God of Deism. In him, key future directions of thought were clearly present.

The Comte de Buffon (1707–1788), Erasmus Darwin (1731–1802), and Jean-Baptiste Lamarck (1744–1829) are labeled "the time voyagers" by Eiseley. He suggests that this trio was especially influenced by "the extraordinary voyage," a literary genre popular in the eighteenth century. Their imaginations stimulated by accounts of noble savages and bizarre societies, these intellectuals were emboldened, says Eiseley, to try "the most dangerous intellectual journey of all—the voyage backward into time" (DC, p. 29). Buffon's vast *Natural History*, resting on the uniformitarian assumptions that had informed Maillet's work, appealed to presently observable natural processes to explain geologic and biologic facts. Foreshadowing the great James Hutton, Buffon ascribed a major causal role to the cumulative effects of rain, winds, frost, and rivers. Accordingly, he projected a greatly lengthened stretch of time in which these subtle forces could produce their impact. Buffon also anticipated Malthus, claims Eiseley, by observing "a tendency for life to multiply faster than its food supply and thus to promote a struggle for existence on the part of living things" (DC, p. 40).

Most important, Buffon formulated an early version of evolutionary theory, holding that "all the races of animals which now exist" have either "degenerated" or "improved" through "an alteration of original constitution" (DC, p. 41). At the same time, Buffon was unable to find a mechanism that would explain *how* evolutionary change took place. This, of course, was Lamarck's great achievement. In his *Zoological Philosophy* (1809), this renowned biologist viewed species as the product of an ages-long developmental process. A drive exists in nature toward greater complexity and perfection of form. The specific forms that emergent life takes, said Lamarck, are determined by an interaction of organism and environment. Eiseley summarizes Lamarck's key idea in this way:

As the world alters, as geographic and climatic areas change, new influences are brought to bear upon plant and animal life. In the course of long ages transformations in this life occur. These alterations are the product of use, of the *effort* which the animal makes to employ those parts which are most serviceable to it under the new conditions. As time passes related species may differentiate further and further from each other and these changes will be retained through heredity. [DC, p. 49]

In short, for Lamarck species are transformed through "the inheritance of acquired characteristics." An unconscious striving to adapt eventually produces inheritable physical change. Erasmus Darwin—grandfather of Charles Darwin, physician, naturalist, and poet—had proposed an identical view in his *Zoonomia* (1794).

Saving the Appearances: Catastrophism

While Lamarckianism would later be rejected by Charles Darwin and his followers, it proved an immensely stimulating and fruitful hypothesis. No less stimulating were the theoretic mistakes of the geologists Abraham Werner (1749–1817) and Georges Cuvier (1769–1832), the two great "catastrophists" of the pre-Darwinian period. Believing that the "history of error" is as significant as the opposite process, Eiseley treats Cuvier with special care and fondness. A professor of natural history in Paris, Cuvier pioneered the field of comparative anatomy. He then applied his immense learning to the problem of interpreting the fossil record, a large chapter of which he himself contributed, through famous digs on the bone-rich Paris basin. To his contemporaries, Cuvier was a poet-sorcerer, "the magician of the charnel house," who from mere fragments of fossil bone could concoct a whole animal. His guiding assumption in this task, reports Eiseley, was that "all anatomical structures [are] so intimately related to the life of the entire creature that no one part can be fitted to perform a certain function without the modification of other related parts" (DC, p. 86). Cuvier's

reconstructions eventually revealed that fossilized remains lie in distinct strata that have been laid down se-
quentially over millions of years. Cuvier's conclusions
were dramatically supported by his English contemporary William Smith, an engineer and surveyor who
showed clearly that each geologic stratum contains a fossil
record peculiar to itself.

The existence of very old, totally extinct worlds of
animal and plant life was now established beyond doubt.
Cuvier, a deeply religious Huguenot, chose to account
for this disturbing fact through an ingenious modification
of the special creation theory. God's creative act, he asserted, had not occurred once, but many times. At the
end of each epoch of creation, a vast cataclysm obliterates
the old and prepares for a newer, more perfect divine
action. Cuvier's view implied, writes Eiseley, that "the
Noachian Deluge is the last in a series of tremendous
upheavals or catastrophes which have separated one world
of prehistoric life from another" (DC, p. 87).

Supported by the authority of the German geologist
Abraham Werner and Cuvier, catastrophism swept all
other theories before it and became orthodoxy. Lost sight
of, observes Eiseley, was the fact that Cuvier's work had
actually destroyed one part of the old Christian world
view while shoring up another. Because of Cuvier's careful anatomical comparisons, the notion of the great chain
of being suffered irreparable damage. There are, he
proved, four main classes of animals (vertebrates, mollusca, articulate, and radiata), and these classes cannot
be placed in an ascending relation to one another. "The
molluscan plan of organs and of adaptations could never
be fitted successfully into a vertebrate sequence," states
Eiseley. Although Cuvier did not recognize its evolu-

tionary implications, he had made the discovery that "there were many stairways of life rather than one" (DC, p. 87; see also DC, pp. 339–341).

Catastrophism had emerged to combat the theories not only of Maillet and Buffon but also of the premier geologist of the eighteenth century, James Hutton (1726–1797). A direct line of intellectual influence runs from Hutton through John Playfair to Charles Lyell and Charles Darwin. The uniformitarian principles of Hutton achieve full vindication in Darwin's work, but Eiseley shows that great though Hutton's achievement was, it also constituted a major intellectual hurdle for evolutionists to overcome.

Darwin and the Overthrow of Uniformitarianism

Not sequential cataclysms but the regular operation of known natural agencies explain the earth's appearance, claimed Hutton. Three grand processes are at work: (1) formation in the ocean of stratified deposits drawn from materials leached from the land; (2) solidification and elevation of these strata by enormous pressures and subterranean heat; (3) fracturing and eroding of the uplifted surfaces by ice, wind, and water. For such processes to manifest their shaping power, vast eons of time are needed. Hutton shocked his contemporaries by proposing that the earth sciences require nothing less than an assumption that the earth is infinitely old. A succession of geologic worlds presents itself, he dramatically stated, with "no vestige of a beginning—no prospect of an end" (quoted in DC, p. 73). But what of the transformations of organic life during these unmeasurable stretches of time? Not only was Hutton silent on this matter, his entire outlook was deeply antievolutionary.

As Eiseley and other commentators have shown, Hutton's temporal sense was cyclical, primarily because of his dedication to the methods of Newtonian science. The three processes he isolates operate to return the earth to an equilibrium condition. Time and raindrops may wear away the mountains, but "productive causes" working on the "unfathomable regions of the sea" give birth to future continents (DC, p. 71). The earth is "a beautiful engine" the laws of whose functioning have now been revealed. But, stresses Eiseley, evolution is neither cyclic nor equilibristic.

Thus, when Hutton's great disciple Charles Lyell tried to solve the species-change mystery he failed, despite having the same clues as his friend Darwin. Lyell understood that there is a competitive struggle in nature; his careful empirical and statistical work with mollusca demonstrated, to the disgruntlement of catastrophists, a continuity of fossilized life in the strata; and, writes Eiseley, "there is clear evidence that Lyell actually anticipated Darwin in the recognition of ecological change which could promote extinction" (DC, p. 102). Moreover, Lyell was keenly aware of the variations that occur within species and bestow competitive advantage and disadvantage. Why then did he not articulate the Darwinian principle of evolution through natural selection? Because, claims Eiseley, Lyell's theoretical bent was too deeply conditioned by Hutton. And this meant that Lyell could see natural selection only as a negative, conserving, balancing process. The "incredibly tight and complicated web of life would, Lyell thought, eliminate immediately any newly emerging creatures which might be evolving through natural means" (FT, p. 52). For Lyell, the war in nature produced extinctions and prevented a given species from growing too numerous—it did not launch successful new creations.

In Eiseley's view, Lyell's failure to solve the evolutionary puzzle symbolizes grave inadequacies in all Newtonian and uniformitarian thought patterns. Productive though these patterns were in overcoming Aristotelian-Christian notions, they enshrined a mechanistic approach to problem solving that was as damaging as it was useful. Dedicated to cyclical, illimitable time perspectives, anxious to find self-sustaining, balancing, and restoring mechanisms, "disinclined to countenance the intrusion of strange or unknown forces in the universe" (DC, p. 114), uniformitarianism essentially taught that life was not going anywhere. So once again, a static view of nature had taken hold. And it was a steep barrier to surmount.

"It was not natural selection that was born in 1859," writes Eiseley. "Instead it was natural selection without balance" (FT, p. 81). Darwin and Wallace saw the world with new eyes. They saw, says Eiseley, that out of the war in nature emerge unpredictable, astonishing new forms of life. Natural selection brings forth wholly unexpected departures: "The common day had turned marvelous. Creation . . . must be even now about us everywhere in the prosaic world of the present" (FT, p. 58). Old arrangements become unbalanced by time; organic life is historic, a story full of surprises that leads not to a single place but in a hundred remarkable directions. Ironically, a crucial element of the old Christian world view stood at the center of Darwin's new synthesis: the sense that time moves as a straight line, developmentally. Darwin's century, then, is for Eiseley the period after 1859, when the full significance of the evolutionary revolution is grasped. It is the era when the essential creativity of time begins to be fully appreciated.

Six Eiseleyan Motifs

His work on *Darwin's Century* served to crystallize Eiseley's entire intellectual outlook. *The Immense Journey*, its
companion volume, vindicated Eiseley's confidence in the
concealed essay as his artistic medium. In these two works,
the whole of his future literary effort lay in concentrated
form. James Schwartz correctly calls evolution "the in-
forming theme" of Eiseley's work, while autobiography
is "the structuring principle."[4] Some shifts in emphasis
and interpretation occur in the later work, but they are
generally not major ones. Throughout, the essays contain
the same essential evolutionary message. There is an outlook which is distinctly and uniquely Eiseleyan, a set
synthesis of ideas and feelings that appears in various
essayistic guises. That synthesis is, we believe, constituted by six distinct perspectives. Together, they are
for Eiseley the meaning of the Darwinian revolution.
We present these here in a condensed, synoptic way. In
the chapters that follow, they will receive close examination.

    1. *Time is immense, linear, and creative.* The evolu-
tionists had demonstrated once and for all that time in
the universe does not run in cycles; nature repeats none
of its performances. Eiseley constantly returns to the title
of Wallace's famous paper, "On the Tendency of Varieties to Depart Indefinitely from the Original Type."
What astronomers had long been suggesting—that galaxies and suns have their own histories—suddenly gained
confirmation in humanity's back yard. Almost simultaneously, the discovery of the second law of thermodynamics demonstrated time's arrowlike character. Natural
selection, a mechanism continuously operating everywhere, revealed a bias in nature toward change and nov-

elty. After Darwin, writes Eiseley, human beings had to adjust themselves "not just to time in unlimited quantities, but *rather to complete historicity, to the emergence of the endlessly new.* . . . Philosophy was to include, henceforth, cosmic as well as organic novelty" (DC, p. 331).

2. *Humanity belongs to the community of descent.* Before the Darwinian revolution, humanity could view itself as the summit of creation, the species specially chosen to sit atop the scale of nature, the image of God. The pre-evolutionary world view emphasized not only the fixity of the types of life but also their essential disconnection. But Darwin and his colleagues envisioned things otherwise: they saw, says Eiseley, "the community of descent of the living world" (IJ, p. 158). Humans discovered written into their own bodies their connectedness with evolving life. If they took evolution seriously, their admiration would be for the total sequence of organic life, not just for one segment of it. Natural selection teases forth a spectacular variety of life forms. Some perish, others persist but change. They are all phantoms, forms assumed by the thread of life. "By this tenuous thread of living protoplasm, stretching backward into time, we are linked forever to lost beaches whose sands have long since hardened into stone" (FT, p. 56). Frederick Elder has suggested that Eiseley's thought is "biocentric" rather than anthropocentric.[5] This term emphasizes that for Eiseley all the manifestations of evolution are kindred and among them none enjoys inherent superiority.

3. *The human brain creates a second world.* Natural selection preserves those organisms that have developed a particularly advantageous part or structure. A species perfects itself only in the limited sense that its characteristics are well adjusted to an ecological niche. But with the emergence of the human brain, nature confronts a structure that has the power to alter its own environment.

By virtue of our expanded cerebral cortex, the world displays language, reflective thought, and planned social action. Perfection ceases to refer to mere adaptibility. For Eiseley, "the achievement of the reasoning brain swings open a possible door to perfection whose story is not told by the limited advantage of a butterfly's wing" (DC, p. 322). Within the human mind a second world blossoms, an inner sky stretches out, dream images play, and reflections of social life combine and recombine. Humanity conceives ideal goals and these create within culture strong new selective forces. Nature now begins "to evade its own limitations in the shape of this strange, dreaming, and observant brain" (IJ, p. 121). Man dwells partly "within a secret universe of his own creation and shares that secret universe in his head with other, similar heads" (IJ, p. 120).

4. *For the evolutionist, the common day has turned marvelous.* A scientist with a sense of wonder—this is the dominant public image of Loren Eiseley, and it is one that he did much to cultivate. Less well understood are the philosophic sources of that sense. What explains Eiseley's great preoccupation with surprise, mystery, the unexpected universe, miracle, the unknown, the secret? Certainly the bent of his personality is a major factor. The student of Eiseley's work quickly recognizes that, temperamentally, this scientist ranks as one of the arch-romantics of our time. But the matter cannot be left there. For Eiseley's talk of how "a strange unexpectedness lingers about our world" (UU, p. 41), proceeds from his conviction that modern science expands rather than reduces the mystery of the world. Evolutionary biology in particular has revealed a tendency in nature toward the wholly unpredictable. Wondrously, every moment witnesses the creation of new life forms. Twentieth-century physics embraces the uncertainty principle, no longer

speaking with Newtonian confidence of eternal natural laws. It predicts less and speculates more. Eiseley argues that if "miracle" means "an event transcending the known laws of nature" and if the theoretical framework which defines natural laws changes each generation, "a little taste for the miraculous in this sense will do us no harm" (FT, p. 171).

5. *Guided by Bacon's ideas, science can serve human ends.* Eiseley continually attacks the view that science reduces the world to the interactions of mechanical forces. Opposed to all forms of materialism, he observes that "men argue learnedly over whether life is chemical chance or antichance, but they seem to forget that the life *in* chemicals may be the greatest chance of all, the most mysterious and unexplainable property in matter" (FT, p. 172). Eiseley is convinced that humanity's greatest danger comes from a materialist philosophy that sees technological development as the highest human activity. He returns to the writings of Francis Bacon to find the proper balance of idealism and materialism. In Bacon, Eiseley sees an admirable humanistic vision, an emphasis on scientific activity as a prelude to the realization of humanity's magnificent potential.

6. *Scientific knowledge bestows neither freedom nor the capacity for love.* Eiseley's essays wrestle with the problem of the scientist as person. Caught up in the great system of evolutionary thought, Eiseley continually inquired into its meaning for him. He refused to adopt a pose of so-called objectivity or to divide his life into scientific and nonscientific departments. By nature merciful and caring, he agonized over the apparent irrelevance of these virtues in "the silent and insatiable war of nature" revealed by the evolutionists (UU, p. 83). He concluded that when one chooses to love—chooses freely and in spite of evolution's grim laws—one defines a world be-

yond the natural. Science does not empower that choice;
rather, individuals bestow such power upon themselves.
As one does so, however, one comes into alignment with
a transnatural force lying at the center of things.

Before examining more carefully how these six motifs
are developed in Eiseley's writing, we must stress that
he was not a systematic thinker. Although these themes
constitute a coherent philosophic position, Eiseley never
sought to work them into a rounded, defensible argument. He cherished the poet's freedom to explore, speculate, and self-contradict. He fulfilled brilliantly the roles
of appreciator, dramatizer, and illustrator. Motifs appear
that harmonize not at all well with these central themes.
One finds unmistakeable longings for death, for cata-
clysmic annihilation of humanity's puny empire, for a
new ice age. Eiseley's innate pessimism warred—often
successfully—with his quest for a ground of hope. Although the clarity, order, and precision of his work suffered thereby, he was able to produce some writings that
are startlingly rich and endlessly suggestive. A great mystic, Loren Eiseley provides us not only with superb meditational literature but also, in a few cases, with pure
experiences of self-transcendence.

4

Creative Time and the Community of Descent

As a communicator of time's vastness, linearity, and unfathomable inventiveness, Eiseley is without peer. Obsessed with measuring every possible ramification of evolution, Eiseley wished to imbue his findings with such artistic power that the everyday consciousness of his readers would be permanently altered. A superb craftsman, he employed image, symbol, anecdote, and narrative structure to create unique temporal impressions. But the way these literary devices were used was determined by some singular patterns of thought and behavior. The most important of these was Eiseley's tendency to personalize evolution, viewing himself as an example of nature's laws and operation. This personalizing movement was an expression of Eiseley's remarkable capacity to identify himself so fully with natural processes and organisms as to lose his own personality. In so doing, he perhaps gained at least a brief victory over time.

There is no better example of this identifying capacity than "The Creature from the Marsh" from *The Night Country*. Like many of Eiseley's essays, this one contains three parts, each of which has its own unity. There are brief narratives in each section as well as reflective and meditational material. Different key symbols appear in all three parts, arranged so as to have a cumulative impact. "The Creature from the Marsh" opens with this characteristic line: "The only thing strange about me is my profession" (NC, p. 153). Extremely proud of his academic discipline, Eiseley nevertheless realized that field anthropologists often appear to be doing puzzling and useless things. Interpreting the work of anthropology to the general public was one of Eiseley's vocations. In this, his great concern was to show how "persons who pursue the farther history of man on the planet earth" often develop a special way of seeing (NC, pp. 153–154). They view the present against the huge panorama of

geologic, evolutionary time. And, says Eiseley here and
elsewhere, this "curious perspective of the archeological
eye" often dislocates, isolates, and torments the seer.

Thus Eiseley walks the streets of a modern city with
its bustle and construction, but he sees only signs of
ruins. With eyes accustomed to exploring "the dead cities
of Mexico—the long centuries wavering past with the
curious distortion of things seen through deep sea water,"
he can only grasp the city as it will necessarily be in some
far future. His wandering has a purpose: "to find a symbol, . . . something that would tell our story to whatever
strange minds might come groping here" (NC, p. 154).
So he weighs "with a quarter-century of digging experience the lasting qualities of metal, stone, and glass"
(NC, p. 154). Tools, flower boxes in tenement windows,
pale blowing leaves of books, "dead television screens,"
"the wilted metal of huge guns," "the curious detached
loneliness of telephone receivers"—these enter and leave
his consciousness.

In a ruined store front, Eiseley finally discovers
among bits of glass "a little cluster of feathers, and under
a shattered pane, the delicate bones of a woman's hand."
Here is his symbol.

Why not? I mused. The human hand, the hand is the story. I
touched one of the long graceful bones. It had come the evolutionary way up from far eons and water abysses only to perish
here. . . . Five hundred million years expended in order that the
shining thread of life could die reaching after a little creation
of feathers in the window of a shop. [NC, p. 155]

There is a tugging at Eiseley's sleeve. The author mentally returns "from some far place," surprised to find his
wife beside him. She wants to enter the shop. There had
been no ruin, but only his vision of it. He sees her in
the shop "pointing, for the benefit of an attentive clerk,

at a little cluster of feathers." As she had parted from
him, Eiseley had "squeezed her slender hand." In a surreal future light, he had seen his wife's skeletal hand.
Panicked, he urges her to postpone her purchase of the
feathers. The episode closes with these words: "It is the
nature, you see, of the profession—the terrible *deja vu*
of the archeologist, the memory that scans before and
after" (NC, p. 156).

Part II of "The Creature from the Marsh" centers
on a black skull brought to Eiseley by visitors who know
nothing of archeology. Like reporters and college fresh-
men, they want to know the monetary value of the artifact
as well as its precise age. Their interview with Eiseley
goes badly. He tries to take them "down that frail ladder
which stretches below us into the night of time" (NC,
p. 157). Unable to make the demanding descent, the
visitors leave Eiseley to his reveries. He had been able
to tell them that the skull is some 5,000 years old, be-
longed to a young woman who had sustained a severe
head injury, and "had not been drawn from a grave."
But he had failed to impart the stupendous factual reality
of the passage of time between the woman's lifetime and
our own. In interpreting the skull, Eiseley had passed
mentally "through ages where water was wearing away
the shape of river pebbles into crystalline sand and the
only sound in the autumn thickets was the gathering of
south-flying birds." The river was much larger then, "an
enormous rolling waste of water and marshes out of which
rose a vast October moon" (NC, p. 157).

Eiseley confesses that, after years of such time traveling, he would practice it even if his livelihood did not
demand it. So sharpened is his time sense that he must
make the journey, striving to "hurl the mind backward
into the wilderness where man coughs bestially and vanishes into the shape of beasts." For he believes this act

of inspecting carefully the shores of time's vast river is uniquely human, an expression of a vision of the human potential that has emerged in the evolutionary process. The human vocation, he concludes, is grasped most clearly by the evolutionist, who knows that the discovery of the way "only lies through man and has to be sought beyond him" (NC, p. 159).

Having introduced the two anatomical symbols of the skeletal hand and the injured skull, in Part III Eiseley develops a third: the footprint of a transitional form of human, which he himself discovered on the shores of a tropical swamp. The forbidding area appeals to him because at the teeming interface of water and land evolution seems very near at hand. Everything "is moving from one element to another, wearing uneasily the queer transitional bodies that life adopts in such places." Land-seeking fish, insect-eating plants, tree-climbing crabs "sit about watching you."

Along drowned coasts of this variety you only see, in a sort of speeded up way, what is true of the whole world and everything upon it: the Darwinian world of passage, of missing links, of beetles with soldered, flightless wings, of snakes with vestigial feet dragging slowly through the underbrush. Everything is marred and maimed and slightly out of focus—everything in the world. [NC, p. 162]

Our normal consciousness is preevolutionary, observes Eiseley. It takes mutable environments like this to remind us that a man is no different from the rest: "His back aches, he ruptures easily, his women have difficulty in childbirth—all because he has struggled upon his hind legs without having achieved a perfect adjustment to his new posture" (NC, p. 162).

Picking his way through a stretch of huge waterlilies, Eiseley mounts a low ridge and discovers a footprint. He had assumed that he was alone. He finds a trail of footprints heading out of the swamp into the interior. The scientist in him causes him to notice that "though undoubtedly human the prints were different in some indefinable way" (NC, p. 163). The shape of the arch implied "an inadequate adjustment to the upright posture"; he pictures the shape of spine and skull. On his knees now, Eiseley excitedly studies the configuration of the toes; the "loose, splayed aspect" of the entire foot "suggested inadequate protection against sprains." The question suddenly arises: "Could it be that I was dealing with an unreported living fossil, an archaic ancestral fossil?" (NC, p. 165).

It occurs to Eiseley to apply the anatomical strategy of comparing ancient and modern forms. He takes off his shoes, and for the first time in his life looks critically at his own feet. He tries to view them as a professional anatomist might. This prompts him to try an obvious experiment. "A little sheepishly and with a glance around me to see that I was not observed, I lowered my own muddy foot into the footprint. It fitted," (NC, p. 165). The marks of the creature from the marsh had simply been left by someone of Eiseley's general size. He had in essence been tracking himself, an evolving creature on an immense journey from water to land: "I was the dark being on that island shore whose body carried the marks of its strange passage" (NC, p. 165).

Eiseley's purpose in "The Creature from the Marsh" is to allow the reader to share, if only briefly, the outlook of the professional archeologist. One suspects that few archeologists have internalized evolutionary perspectives to the extent that Eiseley has; therefore, Eiseley's object is also to invite others to share his own painfully intense evolutionary vision, to experience his "terrible *deja vu.*" In any case, he succeeds brilliantly. The three symbols interact to impart his complex message about time. The skull attests to time's dizzying immensity. Black from "the irons and acids and mineral replacements of ice-age gravels," it "was polished and worn from the alterations of unnumbered years" (NC, p. 156). Although the skeletal female hand—product of five hundred million years—is also emblematic of time's enormous span, it suggests something more.

For the evolutionist, time "pursues an unseen arrow which is irreversible" (IP, p. 16). Governed by the second law of thermodynamics, time moves linearly toward greater randomness. Indeed, emergent disorder is time's chief product and measure. Eiseley's vision of the ruined city is that of modern science, which postulates a final condition of total enervation for the universe. Yet despite this ultimate fate, humans still inscribe gold rings with "for always" and reach longingly for a decorative cluster of bright feathers. Eiseley refused to concede that such indications of our hunger for permanence and beauty are scientifically insignificant. Even the professional archeologist with his "antique reptilian eye" must be moved by the poignant loveliness of his wife's slender hands. His account of human nature must do justice to the human capacity to cherish the evanescent, making a tiny segment of evolutionary time personal.

Finally, the symbol of the footprint communicates in a stunning way the radical meaning of time's creativity. Even the career evolutionist is apt to forget that the organic world around him is a tissue of emergent novelty. Yet his own bodily structures indicate that he also inhabits "the Darwinian world of passage"—he too is a possible specimen of evolutionary change to be examined by future scientific investigators. The idea of the great chain of being still grips the modern mind, shielding it from the terrifying fact that rather than being the summit of creation, humans are potential links to an unpredictable future race. Difficult enough for the intellect, the movement from anthropocentric to biocentric vision taxes the emotions almost to their limits.

"The Creature from the Marsh" is only one among dozens of essays and poems treating these aspects of evolutionary time. "The Snout" (FT) imaginatively recreates that moment three hundred million years ago when the fresh-water Crossopterygian began its career as a terrestrial creature; but Eiseley's concern is to illuminate the present creativity of nature, to show that humans are only one of many expressions of life. "We are not," he stresses, "its perfect image, for it has no image except Life, and life is multitudinous and emergent in the stream of time" (IJ, p. 59).* "How Death Became Natural" (FT), an expository essay on Cuvier, Lyell, and Hutton, contains a remarkable poetic excursus on the "glistening thread" of organic life, which, though linear, has "strange turns in its history, loops and knots and constructions" (FT, p. 56).

"The Angry Winter" (UU) meditates on humanity's indebtedness to recurrent ice ages for its development. Atypically, the long essay communicates a sense of time's immensity less through image and anecdote than through a discussion of glaciation patterns in the Permian, Pleis-

---

*Significantly, Eiseley believed that neither "human" nor "humanoid" life exists anywhere else in the universe. So unique are the earth's environments, so fecund, creative, and multiplistic is organic life, so surprising is "the immense journey" that it is vain to suppose that on another planet "human" forms have appeared. He wrote: "There may be wisdom; there may be power; somewhere across space great instruments, handled by strange manipulative organs, may stare vainly at our floating cloud wrack, their owners yearning as we yearn" (IJ, p. 162). But, he added, this shall not be a *human* yearning: "Of men elsewhere, and beyond, there will be none forever" (IJ, p. 162).

tocene, and Paleozoic geologic epochs. In "How Natural Is 'Natural'" (FT), Eiseley describes a horseback ride over high western mountains and a descent to the desert floor below. As he passes through a sequence of vividly different environments, he realizes that he is on "a journey into eons of the past" (FT, p. 163). He reads the geologic evidence, going farther and farther back in time. This was one of Eiseley's favorite literary strategies. He repeatedly ventured over temporally significant landscapes (see, for example, "The Slit" in *The Immense Journey*), using them as stimuli for imagining the details of vanished geologic epochs. These journeys down what he called "the road of time" allowed him to compress geologic time into a manageable and vivid series of images. He wrote many of these compressed geologic histories, and they make haunting reading.

That his readers might share the evolutionist's peculiar experience of time was Eiseley's fondest artistic hope. He recognized that if he could refashion our consciousness of time, he might also help us appreciate what he called "the community of descent." Evolutionary theory postulates an unbroken sequence of life radiating from primitive organic forms. For Eiseley this idea is infinitely suggestive and, when fully contemplated, properly productive of awe. He chafed in the presence of those who failed to grasp the immense significance of the fleshly continuity of evolving life. Eiseley believed that this continuity calls humanity to no less a task than redefining its relation to the entire nonhuman world. It is even possible to view Eiseley as the modern counterpart of St. Francis of Assisi, preaching the brotherhood of the species and the sacred primacy of created life. Surprisingly, in this context Darwin becomes the founder of the new faith.

Eiseley regarded Darwin as far more indebted to theological influences than is realized. Ostensibly a rigorous and unsentimental scientist in the empirical, skeptical tradition of Francis Bacon and David Hume, Darwin was also a visionary and an artist who drew on the Anglo-American "parson-naturalist" tradition of natural history (DC, p. 13). Eiseley supported this interpretation by a study of Darwin's early notebooks. He was particularly taken with these lines from the 1837 journal:

If we choose to let conjecture run wild, then animals, our fellow brethren in pain, disease, suffering and famine—our slaves in the most laborious works, our companions in our amusements—they may partake of our origin in one common ancestor—we may be all melted together. [quoted in DC, p. 352]

This insight, argued Eiseley, shows us the full measure of the evolutionists' breakthrough. Darwin had grasped that "we may be all netted together in one gigantic mode of experience, that we are in a mystic sense one single diffuse animal, subject to joy and suffering beyond what we endure as individuals" (ST, p. 186).

Eiseley sought to be as literal as possible about the "single diffuse animal" in which all things participate. From his evolutionary standpoint, the separate species called forth as adaptations to particular environments are not the primary reality. Of far greater import is the process itself, which is inseparable from the living substance upon which it works. The process is one terrifically vast branching activity that joins each of its separate manifestations. It is cumulative, so that higher forms contain within themselves traces of the structures and tendencies of lower forms. This means that all mammals experience the world in similar ways, but that they also know the way of the reptile, for it is from this order of life that they evolved. The great modern evolutionary theorist George Gaylord Simpson once remarked that "in a sense the mammals, and the birds too, are simply glorified reptiles. But in a similar sense the reptiles are glorified amphibians, the amphibians glorified fishes, and so on back until all forms of life might be called glorified amebas, and the very amebas could be considered glorified protogenes or protoviruses".[1] This is the starting point for much of Eiseley's thought and art.

Eiseley's frequently anthologized essay, "The Flow of the River," beautifully communicates his vision of the community of descent. Here again Eiseley's power to identify with organic (and even inorganic) processes is vividly apparent. The essay's subject is "common water"— its magical quality, elegant multiformity, life-generating power. Like a modern Thales, Eiseley is moved to metaphysical speculation through his contemplation of water's mysteries: "Its substance reaches everywhere; it touches the past and prepares the future; it moves under the poles and wanders thinly in the heights of air. It can assume forms of exquisite perfection in a snowflake, or strip the living to a single shining bone cast up by the sea" (IJ, p. 16). The essay itself achieves an almost fluid quality through the narration of two episodes involving the great Platte River.

In the first of these, Eiseley tells of overcoming his fears for a brief time (he was a nonswimmer beset with morbid fantasies about drowning) and floating down the slow but treacherous river. Face skyward, he is taken by the great flow and sent "sliding down the vast tilted face of the continent" (IJ, p. 19). Released by grace from his anxieties, he suddenly experiences a myriad of new and profound sensations. Sprouting under him "in dancing springs of sand" is the debris of mountains being carried down to the Gulf of Mexico. He streams over what had

once been great sea beds played upon by giant reptiles.
With "the delicacy of a crayfish's antennae," he touches
his own "margins," feels for the great river fish, senses
in the stranded timber the lingering presence of beaver,
apprehends that the shallows contain broken bits of pioneer wagons and fragments of mammoth bone. He grasps
that he is himself erosion's agent, "wearing down the face
of time and trundling cloud-wreathed ranges into oblivion" (IJ, p. 19).

The experience now becomes "a tremendous adventure." He gives way entirely to this "mother element"
which, even this late in evolutionary time, still spawns
and protects almost every living thing. He undergoes a
"curious absorption," the "extension of shape by osmo-
sis":

I was streaming alive through the hot and working ferment of
the sun, or oozing secretively through shady thickets. I *was* the
water and the unspeakable alchemies that gestate and take shape
in water, the slimy jellies that under the enormous magnifi-
cations of the sun writhe and whip upward as great barbeled
fish mouths, or sink indistinctly into the murk out of which
they arose. [IJ, pp. 19–20]

That water is his essence is communicated to him. Like
turtles and fish, he too is a "watery projection." Humans
are "myriad little detached ponds with their own swarm-
ing corpuscular life"—they are "but a way that water has
of going about beyond the reach of rivers" (IJ, p. 20).
He recalls Thoreau's characterization of the emerald pick-
erel in Walden Pond as "animalized water." Had Thoreau
known of evolution, he would have seen that this animalized water had simply "changed its shapes eon by
eon to the beating of the earth's dark millennial heart"
(IJ, p. 21). With this insight "the great voyage" ends.

The kinship of all species, their common participation in "the water brotherhood," is again the subject of the essay's second episode. Eiseley tells of a wintertime visit to the Platte, where he finds at the edge of a backwater a catfish frozen in the ice. He cuts out a block containing the fish and takes it home. There, to his amazement, the melting ice reveals a very lively creature, "a yellow-green, mud-grubbing evil-tempered inhabitant of floods and droughts and cyclones" (IJ, p. 23). The catfish lived with him all winter. Then, one spring night, it leaped from its tank and suffocated on the basement floor. Perhaps, speculates Eiseley, the fish was bored, felt a migratory impulse, or "felt, far off, the pouring of the mountain waters through the sandy coverts of the Platte." More likely, it behaved as do all of its kind who, when confined to drying shallows, carry the impulse to jump in order to find a deep channel and so survive. Thus, "a million ancestral years had gone into that jump, I thought as I looked at him, a million years of climbing through prairie sunflowers and twining in and out through the pillared legs of drinking mammoth" (IJ, p. 24).

His own vivid river voyage had enabled Eiseley to identify with the catfish as never before. He remembers his own "green extensions, my catfish nuzzlings and minnow wrigglings" (IJ, p. 26). He recalls that some of the catfish's "close relatives" began the experiment with air-breathing of which he is the great beneficiary. Now clear to him is this fact:

We were both projections out of that timeless ferment and locked as well in some greater unity that lay incalculably beyond us. In many a fin and reptile foot I have seen myself passing by—some part of myself, that is, some part that lies unrealized in the momentary shape I inhabit. [IJ, p. 24]

The creation is one, and in it no part enjoys any inherent preeminence. Nature, affirms Eiseley, is certainly ca-

68 *Loren Eiseley*

pable of inventing a being more beautiful than man. What of it? "Having been part of the flow of the river, I feel no envy—any more than the frog envies the reptile or an ancestral ape should envy man" (IJ, p. 25).

The biocentric, unitary perspective of "The Flow of the River" reappears continually in Eiseley's writing. His frequent attempts to discover prehuman tendencies in his own behavior stem from Darwin's notion that "we are all melted together." And that idea motivates some of Eiseley's curious merciful interventions in natural dramas, as when, in "How Natural Is 'Natural'?", he separates a black snake from the raging body of a hen pheasant around which it was coiled. He says of that act that it was not done for knowledge: "Instead, I contained, to put it simply, the serpent and the bird. . . . I had embraced them in my own substance" (FT, pp. 177–178).

In "The Angry Winter", he restrains himself from shooting a jackrabbit caught out in a prairie blizzard. Although he feels their mutual alienness, knows the millions of years of evolutionary time separating them, the intense cold stirs up an ancient affinity. Both creatures survived the Pleistocene glaciations. Once, without knowledge of fire's usage, a human being was like this small "crumbled" beast, trying to endure alone "the blue nights and the howling dark" (UU, p. 119). Eiseley's sympathy goes out to another veteran of the ice.

It should be noted that in Eiseley's poetry this sense of the intense kinship of all life receives continual emphasis. "In the Fern Forest of All Time I Live" does more than compare the narrator's patient, millennial time sense to that of reptiles. It seriously affirms that "I still contain/ a portion of lost lizard blood"; that "this hand was present with the gorgosaver"; that "an anacondine wrench of the genetic code/might well have left/all of mankind still buried in the coal" (IA, pp. 91–92). As it is, our genes still bespeak our reptilian origins. But we betray an anthro-pocentric bias when we state the matter in that way. In "The Fish at Paupak," Eiseley encounters a great gar and learns that "that old gar eye/is in us as in water" (IA, p. 32). More precisely, the fish waits, "containing man as part of his element, not the reverse." By implication, the fish is not here to serve human purposes; rather, both fish and human are equal aspects of the one great organism whose creator is evolution itself.

5

The "Second World" of Human Consciousness

In words that Eiseley might well have penned, the great cultural historian Jacob Bronowski has written, "Every human action goes back in some part to our animal origins; we should be cold and lonely if we were cut off from that blood stream of life." Nevertheless, he points out, "it is right to ask for a distinction: What are the physical gifts that man must share with the animals, and what are the gifts that make him different?"[1] Although Eiseley continually emphasized humanity's fundamental relatedness to the biotic world, he did not—as have some recent thinkers—deny the validity of Bronowski's question. Far from it. Humans occupy for him a special place in nature, and he devoted many pages to the delicate problem of defining that place. Naturally enough, his approach was less that of a philosopher or theologian than of an anthropologist and historian of evolutionary concepts. In Eiseley's discussions of human uniqueness, three ideas predominate: (1) We are "pedomorphic" creatures, whose early life is dramatically conditioned by the requirements of rapid brain development; (2) we occupy a "second" or "superorganic" cultural world, one that exists in its own dimension alongside the nonhuman "first world"; (3) our moral nature is open, a "reservoir of indetermination" (DC, p. 347).

When expounding these concepts, Eiseley writes in a somewhat more technical way than is usual for him, and it is vital that his argument be closely followed. For not only is Eiseley's peculiar form of mysticism partly based upon it, but so also is his bold understanding of humanity's immediate task. Eiseley's analysis leads him to propose a total redirection of the human quest for transcendence. He will call for a new ethic founded upon a new religious and ecological sensibility.

73

Pedomorphism and the Mystery of Human Brain Capacity.

A famous disagreement between Charles Darwin and
Alfred R. Wallace prompts many of Eiseley's specula-
tions on human nature. He recounts the dispute in *Darwin's Century* and interprets its contemporary relevance
in a number of other writings.[2] The question upon which
the quarrel centered was: can the great size of the human
brain be explained in purely evolutionary terms? Because
the skull of modern humans must house a richly con-
voluted cerebrum, it normally achieves a capacity of about
1500 cubic centimeters. The cranial capacity of a gorilla
is only about 450 cc., and that of the extinct tool-using,
upright-walking hominid Australopithecus ranges up to
650 cc. (Neither Darwin nor Wallace knew of the Aus-
tralopithecine family, which came to light only in 1925.)
Is this remarkable difference the result of natural selection?

    Wallace answered no. He argued that a far smaller
brain would certainly have insured human survival. Even
the most "primitive" living humans, observed Wallace,
possess intelligence "very little inferior to that of the
average member of our learned societies" (DC, p. 311).
In *The Origin of Species*, Darwin had stressed the principle
of limited superiority. "Natural selection," he wrote,
"tends only to make each organic being as perfect as, or
slightly more perfect, than the other inhabitants of the
same country with which it had to struggle for existence"
(quoted in DC, p. 310). By this reasoning, the difference
in cranial volumes separating the highest from the next
highest human forms should be very slight. But Wallace

drew attention to humanity's near-total superiority, our
relative perfection. Mathematical intelligence, moral reflection, artistic and musical gifts—in humans, these traits
are far more developed than "necessary" when necessity
is measured by the survival needs of individual and group.
Wallace therefore concluded that "some higher intelligence may have directed the process by which the human
race developed" (quoted in DC, p. 312).

Darwin violently objected to Wallace's "miraculous
addition" to their common theory, and he remained to
the end a firm positivist on this point. In Eiseley's view,
Darwin failed to supply a valid answer to Wallace's queries (IJ, p. 84). Eiseley notes that only major advances in
recovering the fossil record will yield a solution. Darwin's
thesis would be sustained if evidence accumulates pointing to a very ancient date for human emergence. For to
explain the modern large brain, the Darwinian needs "a
long slow competition of human group with human group"
(IJ, p. 91). In the late 1950s, Eiseley believed the data
supported a Wallacean view, namely that "the rise of
man from a brain level represented in earliest preglacial
times by the South African man-apes took place with
extreme rapidity" (IJ, p. 117). In later writings on this
topic—writings that took into account the great finds of
Louis and Mary Leakey—Eiseley did not alter his stance.

But in accepting the swift-tempo view of human
brain development, must one abandon the principle of
natural selection? Eiseley believes not, eschewing Wallace's "mystical direction" (IJ, pp. 119, 90). Whereas a
radically expanded cortex may be only marginally advantageous in a physically brutal competitive environment, there is also for human beings a social reality
demanding adaptive responses. The motivation for early
humans to develop their capacities for well-organized ac-

tion was always strong. Their small size meant that to kill large game animals they would have to band together, an action requiring enhanced communication skills. Cooperative behavior became especially necessary during the great Pleistocene ice ages, whose extreme conditions not only tested the limits of hunting abilities but turned humans to plant domestication. The possibility of an agricultural existence further enhanced the importance of regularized social life. Thus, pressures arose for a human type with enlarged abilities for symbol manipulation. The new struggle in nature was "a struggle for symbolic communication, for in this new societal world communication meant life" (IJ, p. 121).

Thus, hypothesizes Eiseley, "it is likely that the selective forces working on the humanization of man lay essentially in the nature of the socio-cultural world itself" (IJ, p. 120). A high premium was placed on linguistic ability and, accordingly, on larger brain boxes. The new social world favored those individuals who were less enslaved to ancient instincts. The characteristics required for social survival were often the opposite of those needed by the solitary individual in nature. "We are now in a position to see the wonder and terror of the human predicament: man is totally dependent on society," wrote Eiseley (IJ, p. 92).

The clearest proof of this dependency is the human "pedomorphic" or "foetalized" condition. At birth, the brains of all large anthropoids are about the same size. After the first year, however, the human infant's skull will have achieved a capacity three times that of an infant gorilla's (ST, pp. 193–194). This exponential growth pattern continues for the human but not for fellow anthropoids. The price paid for this is a vastly extended childhood, necessary if this huge brain is to "receive,

store, and learn to utilize what it received from others"
(IJ, p. 122).

A human is a "foetal" creature in two senses: the
adult's physical appearance displays characteristics "which
at some earlier stage of evolutionary history were actually
only infantile" (IJ, p. 130); and the playful, inventive
openness of the child survives into a long adulthood.
What provokes and sustains this development is society
itself, where "with every advance in language, in symbolic thought, the brain paths multiplied" (IJ, p. 124).
Eiseley adds, "This is a simplification of a complicated
problem, but it hints at the answer to Wallace's question
of long ago as to why man shows such a strange, rich
mental life, many of whose artistic aspects can have had
little direct value measured in the old utilitarian terms of
the selection of all qualities in the struggle for existence"
(IJ, p. 124).

Eiseley thus proposes that a biological fact was caused
by a specifically social need. If this is so, social phenomena cannot be reduced to their biological basis; on the
contrary, one can correctly think of society as a new
setting for adaptive behavior. And we can even find validity for the old idea of human perfection. Small, advantageous changes in limbs, teeth, fins, and other highly
specific parts insure survival, insisted Darwin. Absolute
species perfection is not possible, for perfection is measured by adaptation to inherently changeable environments. But what if a species that could significantly alter
its own environment emerged? The human brain is a part
of the whole being, to be sure. But when it undergoes
dramatic improvement, the importance of the other human parts dwindles. Keener vision, greater height, larger
lungs—these are useful, but not nearly so useful as an
extra measure of cortex. The ability to reshape environments is enjoyed not by the bigger bodied but by the

bigger brained. Darwin failed to realize, says Eiseley, "that with the shift from the evolution of parts to the evolution of the brain the principle of relative perfection did not rule." Social man is able to dream of an absolute perfection. Observes Eiseley, "Selection then...may have come under the guidance of man's nobler nature" (DC, p. 322).

Evolution in "The Second World"

With the emergence of human beings, "the particulate evolution of biological organs" receded in importance (IP, p. 19). Eiseley attached enormous significance to this development; more then a dozen essays treat the shift from "partitive" to mental evolution. In his view,

just as biological evolution had brought the magic of the end- lessly new in organic form, so the evolving brain, through speech, had literally created a superorganic structure unimag- inable until its emergence. [IP, pp. 18–19]

The mental interaction of humans creates a new, social environment whose real structures are invisible. Once transplanted into this environment, humanity "was being as rigorously selected for survival within it as the first fish that waddled up the shore on its fins" (IJ, p. 120). "Science and the Sense of the Holy" (ST) develops the image of the "invisible niche." Those gifted with "the pedomorphic brain" begin to occupy, says Eiseley, a new type of ecological niche: "a speaking niche, a wondering niche which need not have been first manifested in tools but in family organization, in wonder over what lay over the next hill or what became of the dead" (ST, p. 196). The "real world" has moved inside people's heads. Com- petition in the old sense ("by ax and spear in the war of nature" [IJ, p. 121]) yields to the unceasing struggle of ideas "in that world of streaming shadows forever hidden behind the forehead of man" [IJ, p. 121].*

Eiseley often calls this invisible structure of human consciousness "the second world." It has emerged alongside the "animal" first world "of chameleon-like shifts and forest changes" (IP, p. 24). Whereas the first world dwells in an "eternal present," the second world knows past and future. Instinct and automatism dominate the earlier stage; deliberation and option shape the latter. Original nature is secure but blind; in the new nature insecurity spawns inquisitiveness and wonder (ST, p. 221). In the second world, the impact of society on the individual is profound, whereas in the first world it is weak. Indeed, writes Eiseley, the first human "was not whole, was not made truly human until, in infancy, the dreams of the group... had been implanted in the waiting, receptive substance of his brain" (IJ, p. 121). The second world is endangered by humanity's fantastic powers of imagination—it is "a weird multiheaded universe" populated by visions of gods and demons, obsessed with darkness and the deliveries of the unconscious. The first world, by contrast, is a timeless Eden of pure experience, uncontaminated by determinism.

Most of Eiseley's writings on the second, superorganic realm consider how the brain of the single individ-

*When speaking about the mind in nature, Eiseley frequently sounds very much like the transcendentalist writers he so eagerly consulted. In *The Immense Journey* he wrote: "Nature, one might say, through the powers of this mind, grossly superstitious though it might be in its naive examination of wind and water, was beginning to reach out in the dark behind itself. Nature was beginning to evade its own limitations in the shape of this dreaming and observant brain" (p. 121).

ual evolves stunningly novel perspectives and images. For example, "The Invisible Island" meditates on the creative value of isolation. Eiseley first remarks the difficulty posed by large bodies of land to potential new life forms. On continental fastnesses all the niches are filled, and the web of organic life is too dense to permit the entry of newly emergent creatures. Islands, on the other hand, are apt to offer "doorways to the unexpected, rents in the living web, opportunities presented to stragglers who might be carrying concealed genetic novelty in their bodies" (UU, p. 159). Secluded and less competitive, islands encourage a species to unfold fresh characteristics in response to its new environment. The purpose of Eiseley's analysis is to sensitize the reader to a subtler kind of comparison. For, to Eiseley,

in some such way man arose upon an island—not on a visible oceanic island but in some hidden forest meadow. Man's self-hood, his future reality, was produced within the invisible island of his brain—the island clouded in a mist of sound. [UU, p. 162]

The "mist of sound" is language, that marvelous stimulator and bewitcher of the mind. In language is the source of conceptualization. "The word," writes Eiseley, encourages its bearer to "separate past from present, project the unseen future, contain the absent along with the real, and define them to human advantage" (UU, p. 162). Human minds are thus so many Galapagos Islands; together, knit by language, they are remarkable, fecund sources of novelty.

"The Invisible Island" is typical of Eiseley's use of the second-world notion. In the sermonic essay "The Last Magician," however, he extended the meaning of this idea considerably. His concern here is with contemporary humanity's excessive detachment from the organic first world. Such alienation, he argues, is the inevitable consequence of our prodigious mental capacities. For symbol-using, big-brained Homo sapiens, complete harmony with the natural is out of the question. Language creates a specifically human universe and enables humans to objectify their surroundings, transpose ideas, and recall the past. With signs and ciphers the universe can be probed, with great advantage to humanity. But a sacrifice is exacted: We give away, says Eiseley, "the certainty of the animal that what it senses is actually there in the shape the eye beholds" (IP, pp. 142–143). The human, cultural world is based on "the ghostly symbols moving along the ramifying pathways of the human cortex" (IP, p. 145). We are doomed, therefore, to a perpetual imprisonment in Plato's cave of illusions.

Nevertheless, separation from the first world exists in varying degrees. Simple cultures stand in vital interdependence with the natural. Their mental constructs bind them to its fertilizing, orgiastic power. Totemic animals father the tribes, and animistic faith sees "distinct and powerful spirits in every tree or running brook" (IP, p. 43). Most of humanity has left this condition of close symbiosis. Population density, systematic agriculture, urban existence, the creation of political empires—all have served to develop the human spirit in a different direction. Both a symptom and a cause of the civilizing of the human spirit were the great axial religions—Buddhism, Taoism, Confucianism, Judaism, Platonism. These answered the intensifying needs of the soul. Coming in the first millennium before Christ, they signalled the emergence of the questing individual longing for transcendence.

The message of these religions was a hard one, writes Eiseley. Transcendence requires forsaking the world, "a rejection of purely material goals, a turning towards some inner light" (IP, p. 147). Of the world religions, Christianity offered the severest test: "Here the personalized tribal deity of earlier Judaic thought becomes transformed into a world deity" (IP, p. 147). Charity and humility were to be the Christian's weapons. Its god had poured out his life for all peoples. The Christian ethic, suggests Eiseley, was almost designed to promote frustration by the austere nobility it required of the individual. Inevitably, the failure of the church to transform even its own adherents led to disillusionment. The Enlightenment offered a less noble but more attainable human project. Progress and the subduing of nature became the goal of secular prophets. The yearning for transcendence was sublimated. But secretly disappointed, spiritually driven technologists soon vented their anger on the first world.

We have now entered a new historical epoch, argued Eiseley. The achievements of science have produced staggering environmental chaos. Space flight symbolizes our power yet reveals our radical dependence on the nurturing first world. The further we remove ourselves from it, the more pressing become its claims. "The human cortex, the center of high-thought, has come to dominate, but not completely to suppress, the more ancient portions of the animal brain," Eiseley states (IP, p. 154). We must reconcile ourselves to the living world around us, but not as primitives. The now abandoned self-sacrificial ethics of the great axial religions remain our light. They are deficient only in their too-exclusive emphasis on social and personal relations. Instead, nature itself must be the object of our ethical reflections. Human survival requires an ecological ethic. If man succeeds in this,

he will, perhaps, have created a third world which combines elements of the original two and which should bring closer the

responsibilities and nobleness of character envisioned by the
axial thinkers who may be acclaimed as the creators, if not of
man, then of his soul. They expressed, in a prescientific era,
man's hunger to transcend his own image, a hunger not entirely
submerged even beneath the formidable weaponry and technological triumphs of the present. [IP, p. 155]

We have spoken of Eiseley's unique form of mysticism. The concept of the second world is central to it.
Human cranial development has been so dramatic that
our mental powers are now potentially unlimited. An
unfathomable new inner realm of consciousness has
opened out. Eiseley felt that our exploration of it has only
just begun. Scientific knowledge is but one result of the
exploring; there remain other modes of knowing to uncover. But so impressive have been the results of science
that we are tempted to channel all energies into technology. This Eiseley regarded as fatal, for if science receives the full impact of the human drive for
transcendence, the earth will be endangered. A new in-
nerness must reconcile us to the earth, uniting second
and first worlds into a new symbiosis. We will treat these
ideas further in our discussion of Eiseley's work on Bacon
and the essay "The Star Thrower."

The Human Brain as "An Organ of Indetermination"

Whoever deeply believes in the Darwinian revolution will
be tempted to despair of human nature. The evolutionists
made the simple but stunning discovery that human beings
are animals. Freud, in many ways Darwin's successor,
confirmed the existence of a prehuman level within the
brain. The Enlightenment's optimism about rationality
has disappeared. "We have frightened ourselves with our
own black nature," claims Eiseley. We whisper to our-

selves, "We will trust no one. Man is evil. Man is an animal. He has come from the dark wood and the caves" (DC, p. 345). Knowing now that humanity is merely an evolutionary product who arose "from a late Tertiary anthropoid stock," can we be anything else but disillusioned?

In such essays as "The World Eaters" (IP), "The Time Effacers" (IP), and "Man in the Autumn Light" (IP), Eiseley appears to share and indeed magnify this post-Darwinian pessimism. Scores of poems like "Man in the Long Term" foresee the end of humanity—"no more than an animal"—whose technological victory over the earth is only momentary (AKA, pp. 53–54). But much of Eiseley's despair arises from his sense that the Western world has made a fatal Faustian bargain with machines. Ultimately, Eiseley is neither hopeful nor downcast about human nature, for he regards it as inherently open. To view humanity as fundamentally aggressive is to misinterpret the evolutionary message. Darwin studied the past to learn what forms preceded contemporary species. But the past provides only limited clues to the future, for with the emergence of the second world a quantum step was taken. Most important, the determined behavior of the first world has given way to a marvelous liberty of choice. Borrowing a term from Henri Bergson, the great French philosopher of evolution, Eiseley often refers to the human brain as "an organ of indetermination" whose creativity includes the power of decision making (DC, pp. 350 ff.).

Writes Eiseley, "The mind of man, by indetermination, by the power of choice and cultural communication, by the great powers of thought, is on the verge of escape from the blind control of that deterministic world with which the Darwinists had unconsciously shackled man" (DC, p. 350). The human brain is a specialized organ whose function is to allow the species to escape specialization. All other life forms are caught in "constricted nooks and crannies of the environment" (DC, p. 347). Culture has its own determining forces, but behind these lies the play of human volition. Thus,

man is many things—he is protean, elusive, capable of great good and appalling evil. He is what he is—a reservoir of indeterminism. He represents the genuine triumph of volition, life's near evasion of the forces that have molded it. [DC, p. 350]

6

Ordinary Miracles:
Science and the
Sense of Wonder

"A somewhat unconventional record of the prowlings of one mind which has sought to explore, to understand, and to enjoy the miracles of this world, both in and out of science"—with these words Eiseley described *The Immense Journey*. To anyone familiar with the whole of Eiseley's work, the last phrase is particularly significant. Obedient to his own sense of wonder, Eiseley entered science. He was not disappointed. Wonders and "miracles" he found in abundance. As we have seen, he regarded natural selection as a veritable engine for the production of miracles of a certain sort. But Eiseley's essentially religious and poetic spirit pressed him into trans-scientific domains. His quest for the miraculous led him toward the mystical (a word he despised and a label he rejected) and the surreal. Fred Carlisle has written of Eiseley's "heretical science."[1] To understand the quality of that heresy, one must examine both the scientific miracles he discovered as well and those that occur out of science. This chapter confines itself to the former.

For Eiseley, the modern scientist inhabits an unexpected universe, a world charged with novelty and blossoming with surprise. The discoveries of Darwin, Einstein, and Heisenberg have overturned the self-adjusting systems of Newton and Hutton. Deterministic perspectives had to be laid aside, for "Darwin had introduced into nature not Newtonian predictability but absolute random novelty" (UU, p. 36). Eiseley believed that the human brain could not have been predicted and that its ways are themselves not predictable. Genetics has revealed that "Each one of us is a statistical impossibility around which hover a million other lives that were never destined to be born—but who nevertheless are being unmanifest, a lurking potential in the dark storehouse of the void" (UU, p. 40).

Quantum mechanics and nuclear physics are built

on the assumption that total predictability is a theoretic impossibility. Eiseley felt that the discovery of antimatter particles "raises the question of whether, after all, our corner of the universe is representative of the entire potentialities that may exist elsewhere" (UU, p. 37). The special quality of the earth's atmosphere "appears to be a product of a biological invention, photosynthesis, another random event that took place in Archeozoic times" (UU, p. 37). We must assume, he argued, that if life exists on other worlds, it is radically different from our own. Those who ease our fears with images of "little men from Mars" are covert Newtonians. Quips Eiseley, "I would be much more willing to consider the possibility of sitting down to lunch with a purple polyp, but even this has anatomical comparisons with the life of this planet" (IJ, p. 159).

If "miracle" or "marvel" mean the interruption of regularity—the appearance of things totally unexpected—then modern science reveals a miraculous universe. Indeed, it offers us a reality one of whose inner laws is randomness.* But there is more. For Eiseley, miracle is also a matter of vision, radically novel perspective, daring extrapolation, extensive connection. The

*In *The Man Who Saw Through Time*, Eiseley wrote: "Physicists, it now appears, are convinced that a principle of uncertainty exists in the submicroscopic realm of particles and that out of this queer domain of accident and impact has emerged, by some kind of mathematical magic, the sustaining world of natural law by which we make our way to the bank, the theatre, to our homes, and finally to our graves. Perhaps, after all, a world so created has something still wild and unpredictable lurking behind its more sober manifestations. It is my contention that this is true, and that the rare freedom of the particle to do what most particles never do is duplicated in the solitary universe of the human mind" (MWS, p. 101).

fully alert scientific mind operates just this way, and so miracles appear to it. "The Judgment of the Birds," arguably his greatest prose achievement, demonstrates these special traits. The essay recounts four "natural revelations" all having to do with birds. In each, rather ordinary incidents pass through the prism of scientific understanding and emerge transformed.

The first two experiences offer convincing proof that a "bird's eye view" of the world is humanly attainable. In the first, Eiseley witnesses a rare moment when, in the predawn stillness, white-winged pigeons pour "upward in a light that was not yet perceptible to human eyes" to take over the spires of Manhattan. The wings of the flocking birds form a "city of light" that tempts Eiseley to "launch out into that great bottomless void" and "go away over the roofs in the first dawn" (IJ, p. 166). In the second incident, Eiseley stumbles toward his morning train, fighting a dense fog. Suddenly, a pair of immense black wings and a huge beak flash in his face. He had almost been struck by a great crow lost in the fog. Knowing that crows rarely fly low near people, Eiseley realizes that the bird had become disoriented. The near collision, the bird had to "assume," took place in his usual flight zone, a hundred feet above the roof lines. Thus, speculates Eiseley, the crow must have experienced a ghastly vision: "desecrating the very heart of the crow kingdom, a harbinger of the most profound evil a crow mind could conceive of—air-walking men" (IJ, p. 169).

The miracles here arise from "border shifting," says Eiseley. In both cases, another world comes into view because things are suddenly seen from "an inverted angle" (IJ, p. 167). The sharp, curious vision of the naturalist was needed to bring these two particular miracles into focus. However, the third requires the trained understanding of the professional paleontologist. Carrying a knapsack "heavy with the petrified bones of long-vanished creatures," Eiseley trudges over the Nebraska Badlands. The hour is late on a cold, "wind-bitten" autumn day. Around him, in what was once a green and lively place, stretches indescribable desolation. "Nothing grows among its pinnacles; there is no shade except under great toadstools of sandstone whose bases have been eaten to the shape of wine glasses by the wind" (IJ, p. 170). Like the Valley of the Kings in Egypt, these *mauvaises terres* are a mausoleum. The ash of old volcanic eruptions still sterilizes the soil; the waste's hues "are the colors that flame in the lonely sunsets on dead planets." Eiseley moves more quickly, anxious to reach camp before nightfall.

It was then that I saw the flight coming on. It was moving like a little close-knit body of black specks that danced and darted and closed again. It was pouring from the north and heading toward me with the undeviating restlessness of a compass needle. It streamed through the shadows rising out of monstrous gorges. It rushed over towering pinnacles in the red light of the sun, or momentarily sank from sight within their shade. Across that desert of eroding clay and wind-worn stone they came with a faint wild twittering that filled all the air about me as those tiny living bullets hurtled past into the night [IJ, p. 171].

A tumultuous singing of south-flying warblers. Impressive enough, but as he stood in the midst of that dead world at sunset it struck Eiseley as utterly miraculous. Why? He saw the birds as fleshly expressions of a stupendous natural process. Their presence suddenly made numinous the dead ground under his feet. He recalls that fifty million years ago bellowing monsters had moved "in a green world now so utterly gone that its very light was travelling on the farther edge of space" (IJ, p. 171).

Around him, he realizes, still lay "the shearing molars of dead titanotheres, the delicate sabers of soft-stepping cats, the hollow sockets that had held the eyes of many a strange, outmoded beast" (IJ, p. 171). They are gone to chemicals. In the eroding stone, "the carbon that had driven them ran blackly." "Dark, savage brains" were now present as salts and metal oxides. "The iron did not remember the blood it once moved within, the phosphorus had forgot the savage brain" (IJ, p. 172). Significantly, Eiseley never speaks of this ancient life as being reduced to chemicals. Rather, it has ebbed from the combinations that gave it vitality.

He lifts up a fistful of the soil, holding it as the birds stream over him. "There went phosphorous, there went iron, there went carbon, there beat the calcium in those hurrying wings," he exults. In the bodies of the warblers the ancient life has somehow been gathered up and reconstituted. The same chemicals whose combinations steadied reptilian monsters now metabolize fleet birds.

Alone on a dead planet I watched that incredible miracle speeding past. It ran by some true compass over field and waste land. It cried its individual ecstasies into the air until the gullies rang. It swerved like a single body, it knew itself and, lonely, it bunched close in the racing darkness, its individual entities feeling about them the rising night. And so, crying to each other their identity, they passed away out of my view. [IJ, p. 172]

The moment ends when Eiseley drops his handful of dirt. He recalls that other humans have come here before him seeking visions in this place. Having received his own, he makes his sign to the darkness: "It was not a mocking sign, and I was not mocked" (IJ, p. 173).

This is a convincing demonstration of how authentic wonders are offered to the scientific mind. Eiseley's work teems with other such evidences, some of them on an artistic par with "The Judgment of the Birds." In the best of them, scientific explanation and literary inventiveness merge perfectly. The reader experiences awe, but always because of, not despite, the information presented. "The Secret of Life" (IJ), "The Great Deeps" (IJ), "How Flowers Changed the World" (IJ and ST), "Easter: The Isle of Faces" (ST), and "The Fire Apes" (ST) all lead the reader through scientific material; the instruction is uncompromising, yet when it ends, "the queerness of the world" suddenly stands revealed and our tendency to take things for granted is arrested.

A literary marvel in its own right, "How Flowers Changed the World" provides another vivid example of how, under the gaze of the evolutionist, "the common day turns marvelous" (FT, p. 58). The essay's subject is the angiosperms, that class of vascular plants whose seeds are enclosed in hard cases. The first true flowering plants, the angiosperms appeared late in evolutionary time. Eiseley explains the critical role these came to play in terrestrial food chains; also, he shows the causal relation between the angiosperms and the rise of warm-blooded animals. In the hands of a less gifted scientific expositor, this topic might generate a merely interesting paper. But caught in the high-power lens of Eiseley's mind, angiosperms become the metaphor for nature's unfathomable creativity. Despite digressions, Eiseley in fifteen short pages imparts a synoptic view of evolutionary history, a lucid clarification of several key adaptive mechanisms, and a curious impression that somehow he actually witnessed the blossoming of the first flower.

For Eiseley, as we have noted, science reveals wonder partly because it affords its disciples unexpected angles from which to view reality. In the opening section of "How Flowers Changed the World," Eiseley bids us "observe the Earth from the far side of the solar system over the long course of geological epochs" (IJ, p. 61). So positioned, we see brown, yellow, and blue stretches of barrenness slowly turn green as simple plant forms "crept upward along the meanderings of river systems and fringed the gravels of forgotten lakes" (IJ, p. 62). Eiseley reminds us that these early "green marchers" did not reproduce by seeds but by the less efficient mechanism of water-borne sperm. Therefore, no flowers were present. For some two billion years, "wherever one might have looked, from the poles to the equator, one would have seen only the cold dark monotonous green of a world whose plant life possessed no other color" (IJ, p. 63).

With great dramatic effectiveness Eiseley dissolves this global picture into a "close-up" of coldblooded existence in the Mesozoic period. A quarter of a billion years ago, reptiles great and small dominated the warm landscape. Eiseley depicts it as "a world in slow motion," limited by the low metabolism of its inhabitants. In it, "tyrannosaurs, enormous bipedal caricatures of men, would stalk mindlessly across the sites of future cities and go their slow way down into the dark of geologic time" (IJ, p. 64). Life dumbly unfolds in a low-oxygen-consumption regimen. He explains how high metabolism frees an animal from the tyranny of the weather. Instead of enduring temperature extremes through hibernation or evasion, creatures with uniform body temperatures (warm-blooded) always remain mobile and mentally alert. But maintaining high metabolism requires food in concentrated forms. While mammalian life marginally existed on the floras of the age of reptiles, it could not flourish. The ideal sustenance for mammals lay in the future. "They were waiting for what flowers, and with them the true encased seed, would bring," says Eiseley. Meanwhile, in nature, all is stiff, formal, upright and green, monotonously green. There is no grass as yet; there are no wide plains rolling in the sun, no tiny daisies dotting the meadows underfoot. There is little versatility about this scene; it is, in truth, a giant's world. [IJ, p. 68]

Rather than proceed directly to the climax of this great saga, Eiseley interposes a vignette designed to heighten appreciation for the vast change the angiosperm would introduce. A sharp, rending explosion—"as though an unwary foot had been put down on a wine glass"— brings him from sleep. He prowls the apartment, suspecting an intruder. Finally, he finds scattered over the rug some small button-shaped objects, hard and polished, and "ribbon-like strips of velvety-green." The mystery is solved. Some days earlier, Eiseley had brought in several wisteria pods. "They had chosen midnight to explode and distribute their multiplying fund of life down the length of the room." Remarkably, a pine cone lying near them had been blown several feet. Over evolutionary time, "a plant, a fixed rooted thing had devised a way of propelling its offspring across open space" (IJ, p. 69). The angiosperms are the great travelers, he recalls. With wings, hooks, spikes, and thistledown mounting on the winds, they are a million times cleverer than their "antiquated cousins, the naked seeds on the pine cone scales" (IJ, p. 69). This nocturnal explosion is merely the echo, he sees, of that explosion of growth a hundred million years ago when the angiosperms finally got a foothold in the world.

The flowers bloomed first in the Cretaceous epoch, assisted by the same cooling of the world's climate that helped doom the great reptiles, dependent as they were on tropical temperatures. Eiseley details the evolutionary stages of this remarkable innovation, stressing the adaptive importance of the encased seed, grown protectively

within the plant. Initiated by a fertilizing pollen grain
not dependent on external moisture, the seed, unlike the
spore, "is already a fully equipped *embryonic plant* packed
in a little enclosed box stuffed full of nutritious food" (IJ,
p. 71). Dressed in its travel-promoting guises, this agent
of reproduction spread the flower forms with amazing
rapidity. To ensure pollination and the nurture of its
seeds, the angiosperms evolved elaborate systems, many
of which constituted new food sources for insects, birds,
and mammals. Nectars and pollens, fruits and seeds, all
provided high-energy starches, proteins, and fats for existing and potential life forms.

Eiseley's language celebrates the multiformity of this
accidental wonder:

All over the world, like hot corn in a popper, these incredible
elaborations of the flowering plants kept exploding. . . . The
flowers bloomed and bloomed in ever larger and more spectacular varieties. Some were pale unearthly night flowers in-
tended to lure moths in the evening twilight, some among the
orchids even took the shape of female spiders in order to attract
wandering males, some flamed redly in the light of noon or
twinkled modestly in the meadow grasses. Intricate mechanisms splashed pollen on the breasts of hummingbirds, or
stamped it on the bellies of black, grumbling bees droning
assiduously from blossom to blossom. Honey ran, insects multiplied, and even the descendants of that toothed and ancient
lizard-bird had become strangely altered. Equipped with prod-
ding beaks instead of biting teeth they pecked the seeds and
gobbled the insects that were really converted nectar. [IJ,
p. 73]

Earlier Eiseley had mused that humanity itself lurked
unborn in the resistant seed case of a wild grass. The
final pages of "How Flowers Changed the World" chron-
icles ("like a speeded-up motion picture") the development of humankind. The great savannahs of the earth,

with their thousands of species of grass now sustained the herds upon which humans would depend. Eventually humans would seize a handful of grass seed and contemplate its domestication. The idea of wheat and with it civilization "would glimmer dimly there." Later, science would remind humanity of its debt to flowers. Without flowers, "archaeopteryx, the lizard-bird, might still be snapping at beetles on a sequoia limb; man might still be a nocturnal insectivore gnawing a roach in the dark" (IJ, p. 77). Like all the great nature poets and ecological seers, Eiseley comprehends humanity's dependence on all that lies below it on the pyramid of life. "The weight of a petal," he concludes, "had changed the face of the world and made it ours" (IJ, p. 77).

Like other of Eiseley's essays, "The Judgment of the Birds" and "How Flowers Changed the World" have deeply affected a generation of readers. The most sensitive of these readers reappraise their entire understanding of matter. They ask what manner of creatures have shared the atoms from which they themselves are constituted. They study the shapes of spaces between birds in flight and consider the mean altitudes of crows. Of interest to them, suddenly, are varieties of seed pods or the reasons for the dental configurations in their own mouths. Eiseley sought this effect. To dwell every moment in the reality of evolution was his goal. Early on, he expunged in himself his ordinary consciousness. His essays, without sacrificing technical accuracy, lure the lay reader into the scientific domain Eiseley himself could not leave.

One might write at great length on the other miracles within science Eiseley uncovered. For example, on several occasions Eiseley surveys the world from the vantage point of a blood cell in the human body. In "The Cosmic Prison," after a superb imaginative excursion of this sort, he asks, "What if the far galaxies man observes make up across void spaces of which we are atomically composed, some kind of enormous creature or cosmic snowflake whose exterior we will never see?" (IP, p. 34).[2] The abiding miracle of organization in the universe is a theme Eiseley developed many times. He believed that this organizing principle "is not strictly the product of life, nor of selection" (IJ, p. 26). In *Darwin's Century*, he criticized the philosophical materialists who used evolution to support their case. When one reduces life to pure atoms, life's most imponderable mystery is thrown out: its tendency to collect itself into ordered wholes (DC, pp. 336, 349). We observe a strange pressure toward higher and more complex structure in organic nature, says Eiseley. He made this fact the basis of several fine pieces, of which "The Secret of Life" (IJ) is the best.[3] The last sentence of that work nicely captures Eiseley's view that from no part of the material universe has life, with its astonishing impetus towards order, absented itself.

I would say that if "dead" matter has reared up this curious landscape of fiddling crickets, song sparrows, and wondering men, it must be plain even to the most devoted materialist that the matter of which he speaks contains amazing, if not dreadful powers, and may not impossibly be, as Hardy has suggested, "but one mask of many worn by the Great Face behind". [IJ, p. 210]

7

For the Uses of Life: Eiseley's Defense of Bacon

Eiseley's popular essays did not enjoy universal acclaim in academic circles. Some of his colleagues thought Eiseley was wasting his time and talent by submitting pieces to *Harper's*, *Esquire*, or *The Atlantic Monthly* (see MWS, p. 104). Others were disturbed by Eiseley's seeming impatience with certain scientific assumptions and procedures. Eiseley was aware that neither *The Immense Journey* nor *The Firmament of Time* offered "science in the usual sense" (IJ, p. 13). Of the former, he said: "I have given the record of what one man thought as he pursued research and pressed his hands against the confining walls of scientific method in his time" (IJ, p. 13). In the essay "How Natural is 'Natural'?" Eiseley referred to "the world beyond the nature that we know," to "that inexpressible realm in which the words 'natural' and 'supernatural' cease to have meaning," and to a knowledge deeper than scientific understanding (FT, pp. 177, 179). These phrases, he later reported, "raised the hackles of some of my scientifically inclined colleagues, who confused the achievements of their disciplines with certitude on a cosmic scale" (UU, p. 31; ST, p. 277).

Eiseley had long prided himself on being the source of intriguing heresies in science. But in the late 1960s, the heretic appeared to have entered a new, antiscientific phase. The strange, existentialist essay, "The Star Thrower" spoke of "the renunciation of my scientific heritage" (UU, p. 86). In *The Invisible Pyramid* collection, issued in 1970, science and technology received harsh treatment. His mood a mixture of alarm and despair, Eiseley contrasted the wise, analogic, religious outlook of native Americans with that of the Western world. The Faustian Western individual—creator of centerless, befouled, violent cities—is analytical, impatiently futuristic, mercilessly secular. He or she studies nature in order to manipulate it and prefers "instruments of power" to "the inventions of calm understanding" (IP, p. 92). Mastery of the external world varies inversely with gaining of social mastery.

And science is the Westerner's engine. A solver of problems, science also creates problems "in a genuinely confusing ratio":

They escape unseen out of the laboratory into the body politic, whether they be germs inured to antibiotics, the waiting death in rocket silos, or the unloosed multiplying power of life. [IP, p. 92]

Eiseley was particularly appalled by the maturing alliance of science with big industry, advertising, and militaristic government. He decried the fact that "the laboratory and its priesthood take an increasing share of the profits as they become a necessity for business survival" (IP, p. 104). That scientists should knowingly foster pollution-generating industrial processes Eiseley found shocking. Their obvious usefulness in the fiendish world of weapons manufacture sickened him. The dreams of Francis Bacon, the great prophet of science, had become nightmares. Ironically, the authority of science grows in proportion to the deterioration of the environment its inventions bring about. "Thus science, as it leads men further and further from the first world they inhabited, the world we call natural, is beguiling them into a new and unguessed domain" (IP, p. 106). Eiseley's language was never more acerbic: under the guidance of science, humanity had become "a world eater," "a slime mold organism," a "time-effacer."

The Invisible Pyramid bears the marks of its era. Almost simultaneously, Americans experienced humiliating defeat in a morally dubious war, the sudden realization of environmental degradation, unparalleled racial bitterness, loosening generational bonds, urban decay, and

terrorism. Eiseley's rhetoric rose to match the demands
of the time. Like Paul Ehrlich, Garrett Hardin, Barry
Commoner, and other radical biologists, he felt called
upon to defend the planet from industrialized science, "a
mechanism which threatens to run out of control" (IP,
p. 105). His unmeasured language could certainly leave
the impression that Western science per se needs to be
foresworn, that a rejection of "technological time" in favor of "the magic of genuine earth time" must be made,
and that the thought forms of primitive cultures should
be recovered (IP, p. 111). And Eiseley's penchant for
literary maledictions and melodramatic prophecies did
not help matters. "The fruition time of the planet virus
is at hand," he proclaimed. "It is high autumn, the autumn before winter topples the spore cities" (IP, p. 71;
see also pp. 70 and 107).

But despite unquenchable inner bitterness as well
as a barely controllable urge to anathematize most things
modern (see, e.g., MWS, pp. 106–108), Eiseley did not
renounce science. Nor did he embrace one of the many
neoprimitivist philosophies of the moment. A careful
reading of *The Invisible Pyramid* and succeeding works
shows no essential deviation from the view of science
developed in the more optimistic years. The essence of
that view is that scientists (and their admirers) are constantly tempted to overestimate the explanatory power
of their hypotheses. When this temptation is succumbed
to, science loses its playful, awestruck, wondering spirit
and dreams of exercising total control over nature. The
will to control in turn robs scientists of their inner life.
It focuses their attention on external processes, commits
them to a pose of so-called objectivity, and forbids them
to treat nature as a personality. For Eiseley, the true
scientist carries a vulnerable spirit into scientific work.
Once a posture of invulnerability is adopted, all is lost.

Obsessed with mechanical, utilitarian progress, science becomes a demonic force.

Eiseley's alarm, then, grew from his conviction that establishment scientists had lost sight of their true mission. That mission, he came to believe, had been beautifully described by Francis Bacon almost four hundred years ago. In *Darwin's Century*, Eiseley included a short digression on two opposed traditions in natural history. The Baconian influence stressed a rigorous, experimental, causal approach to nature. The opposing humanistic tradition drew strength from such early parson-naturalists as John Ray, Gilbert White, and William Paley. These men patiently observed and inquired about nature because they found it an avenue to God. From them flowed a literary tradition that Thoreau, W. H. Hudson, and Ernest Thompson Seton embellished and extended (DC, pp. 10–16).

Eiseley later developed a series of lectures on Bacon. These first appeared in book form in 1961; in 1973 an expanded version of the work was issued with the title *The Man Who Saw Through Time*.[1] Significantly, the earlier distinction between two sorts of natural history is abandoned. After a careful study of Bacon, Eiseley concluded that "the Lord Chancellor" had grasped science's real possibilities in a vision no less humanistic than that of the "parson naturalists."

That Eiseley should have written so extensively on Bacon is surprising, for to many historians and social critics, Bacon symbolizes the evil tendencies that Eiseley abhorred. They see in his writings the source of our fascination for transforming the environment with ever-larger tools. Bacon, they charge, inspired his followers to attack the natural world with cold, methodical intellect—to refashion it to human purposes through great collective endeavors. In 1971, Eiseley acknowledged that

"Today the 'great machine' that Bacon so well visualized,
rolls on, uncontrolled and infinitely devastating, shaking
the lives of peoples in remote jungles of Vietnam as it
torments equally the hearts of civilized men" (MWS, p.
96). Yet, believed Eiseley, the real Bacon has been car-
icatured, diminished, distorted. His works contain a wise
understanding of the proper limits of science as well as
a vivid sense of its proper end.

Bacon's key ideas have long since become common-
places.* So obvious do they seem that we fail to appreciate either their relative novelty or enduring richness.
Yet, as Eiseley observed, Bacon's new definitions of culture and inventiveness were so alien to his contemporaries
that he encountered a communication problem as recon-
dite as that later faced by Darwin (MWS, p. 14). It is
from Bacon that we have learned to expect scientific ac-

---

*An exact contemporary of Shakespeare, Bacon remained
at the center of English political power most of his life. Born
into a noble and influential family, he early caught the attention
of Elizabeth I because of his remarkable intellect. He followed
a legal career, became close friends with the much-favored Earl
of Essex, received from him a huge estate, and, when Essex
and the queen quarreled, attempted to reunite them. In this he
failed. And then, in one of those acts which make him so
controversial, he accepted the queen's order to prosecute Essex.
The trial resulted in Essex's execution. Under James I, Bacon
rose to great rank, but only after ordering the torture of a
prisoner to obtain a confession. For this, he was denounced by
the great champion of common-law rights, Sir Edward Coke.
By the time Bacon was sixty, he held the office of Lord Chancellor. Then, almost overnight, he lost everything. Caught accepting a bribe from a litigant, Bacon confessed and was deprived
of all his offices. In his few remaining years he worked to
complete his writings on the advancement of science, which he
had begun publishing in 1605.[2]

tivity to help in "the relief of man's estate." In its time, that was a radical idea. Philosophers disputed all topics, including nature, with truth as their objective. Bacon recognized that the truths emerging from the researches of Galileo and Kepler were of a different order than those available from Plato, Augustine, or St. Thomas. Activist, experimental, and instrument-assisted, these studies promised to provide highly practical inventions and cumulative processes.

Like Descartes, Bacon taught the Western mind the value of doubt. Our eagerness for certainty, he vividly showed, prevents us from building up a store of well-tested, dependable truths. Because certain "Idols," or deceptive tendencies, dominate the human mind, knowledge does not easily and automatically advance. One such tendency is our persistent failure to recognize that we never perceive the world directly and cleanly. Rather, our view is always partial—conditioned both by our inner demands for order and our feelings. Another tendency is for the human observer to see reality only in terms of pet theories. The mind in effect tunes out all other signals than those it is poised to hear. Finally, Bacon remarked the truth-obscuring powers of both words and dogmatic systems. Language, he warned, is elusive, and its users are tempted to make words into real things. (This insight, of course, has become the foundation of much contemporary Anglo-American philosophy.)

These idols will be banished, claimed Bacon, if humanity gains new respect for the vast complexity and range of nature. Past philosophers, he complained, erected great systems on the basis of scanty evidence. The lesson of Galilean science is that in order to know the world, one must first become childlike, humble, unprepossessed. Eiseley was fond of this statement from Bacon's *The Parasceve*:

For the world is not to be narrowed till it will go into the
understanding (which has been done hitherto), but the understanding is to be expanded and opened till it can take in the
image of the world. [quoted in MWS, p. 9]

This attitude, of course, is merely a starting point. To
take in the whole image cannot be the hope of one person.
Gigantic as it is, nature will reveal its secrets only after
centuries of empirical study.

The enormity of the task, insisted Bacon, requires
altogether new social institutions. Natural philosophy,
to be productive, must be an organized, systematic, cooperative venture. In his *New Atlantis*, Bacon created an
imaginary society dominated by a college of science. He
urged James I to found such an enterprise, and in many
ways the great Royal Society that emerged not long after
his death was his child. Bacon believed that if such or-
ganizations were to flourish, and if the level and quality
of experimental and mathematical activity could be dramatically increased, humanity might enter a new era. Its
keynote and theme would be nothing less than the total
mastering of nature. The haphazard development of the
practical arts would give way to a deliberate fashioning
of an "artificial nature." "Another universe or theater of
things" (MWS, p. 53) would come into view.

Benjamin Farrington calls Bacon "the philosopher
of industrial science."[3] Bacon saw himself as the inventor
of a great political-cultural "engine" which would "discover what nature does or may be made to do" (MWS,
pp. 32–34). These phrases ring ominously in contemporary ears. Should we not regard Bacon as the father
of our heedless mechanized quest for modernization? Is
it not naive to propose, as Bacon did, an unchecked part-
nership between big science and strong, centralized national governments? Do we not detect intolerance toward

tradition, social life, organic community, pristine nature? What ends are being served by this engine, and are human beings good enough to run it? In short, aren't Bacon's formulae the very essence of that Faustian spirit that Eiseley so vigorously denounced?

Eiseley attributes such questions to an incomplete understanding of Bacon. Bacon's mother was a staunch Puritan, his father a skilled politician; his intellectual environment was formed by Calvin and Shakespeare. Predictably, Bacon was no frivolous utopian. "He knew," says Eiseley, "that man himself, unless well-studied and informed, was part of the darker aspect of that unknown country, which, as he said, 'awaited its birth in time'" (MWS, p. 63). Integral to Bacon's outlook was the traditional belief that "all things are in truth biformed and made up of a higher species and a lower" (MWS, p. 100). This means that man is inherently double: part brute, part human.

Eiseley recounts a terrifying boyhood experience that provided him with a graphic symbol for this Baconian perception. As he walked a dark, rain-blown country road, a huge racing hay wagon surprised him from behind. High atop it rode the dark figure of a farmer. Then a bolt of lightning lit up the scene and Eiseley saw in the man's face something unutterably grotesque.

It was—by some fantastic biological exaggeration—two faces welded vertically together along the midline, like the riveted iron toys of my childhood. One side was lumpish with swollen and malign excrescences; the other shone in the blue light, pale, ethereal and remote—a face marked by suffering, yet serene and alien to that visage with which it shared this dreadful mortal frame. [MWS, p. 114]

In that instant, says Eiseley, "I saw the double face of man." We are, as Bacon realized, "diseased and fungoid, with that pale half-visage of nobility and despair dwarfed but serene upon a two-fold countenance" (MWS, p. 115).

Sober though he was about human nature, Bacon nevertheless refused to succumb to pessimism. He possessed, claims Eiseley, an uncanny sense of time's vastness and the latent possibility in things. Indeed, in Eiseley's treatment Bacon emerges as a proto-evolutionist. Armed with the conviction that carefully structured institutions (especially educational ones) might allow a maximization of humanity's inventive power, Bacon viewed human beastliness as a challenge rather than a barrier. He also held that humanity's ethical and creative capacities might themselves be scientifically studied. Bacon's second world (Eiseley's own concept is patterned on Bacon's) was to be "a world of men transformed, not merely men as we know them amidst the machines and pollution of the twentieth century" (MWS, pp. 56–57; see also p. 98). Surprisingly, Bacon did not necessarily prefer those scientific projects that promised to yield only technical power. Though he deserves the title of "prophet of industrial science," his sense of the possible scope of scientific work was very great (MWS, p. 98). A "science of the spirit" is a phrase Bacon would readily have understood.

But most important, Bacon never lost sight of the purposes to be served by his great "engine." *The Advancement of Learning*, claims Eiseley, eloquently manifests Bacon's concern "not only with knowledge, but its application for human benefit and freedom." Eiseley continually returns to this statement of Bacon's vision:

Mere power and mere knowledge exult human nature but do not bless it. We must gather from the whole store of things such as make most for the uses of life. [MWS, p. 63]

Modern science, Eiseley believed, is more dedicated to

the uses of death than life. Bacon's delicate vision, his evolutionary hope, has been sacrificed to a purely materialist conception of progress. Throughout his writings, Eiseley bemoaned the excessive attention we pay to mastering the external environment. Had we listened better to Francis Bacon, he implies, our experimental activity would aim more at the production of great souls and imaginative spirits. Bacon is rooted in the Renaissance; he shared its exuberant confidence in human powers and the possibility of their expansion. But he goes beyond the aristocratic humanism of the Florentines. Bacon's emphasis on the inherently collective nature of scientific progress is entirely democratic. He foresaw a wholly new social order—one in which the scientific habit of mind is universal, the production of the humanly useful is a society-wide preoccupation, and the second, cultural, world expresses both human rationality and charity (MWS, p. 89).

It should be noted that, in his search for science with a human face, Eiseley not only came to Bacon's defense but also attempted to exonerate the shapers of the parson-naturalist tradition. Often dismissed by positivistic scientists as too soft, literary, or undisciplined, writers such as Gilbert White, Coleridge, Emerson, Melville, Thoreau, John Burroughs, and Richard Jefferies are far from scientifically irrelevant, believed Eiseley. In *Darwin's Century* he makes much of Charles Darwin's intellectual debt to White (DC, pp. 13–14). The late essay "Man Against the Universe" measures Romanticism's part in the Darwinian breakthrough. Darwin's mind, argues Eiseley, was shaped and readied by the "romantic current" that swept over him in his youth (ST, p. 214). Keats, in his 1818 poem "Epistle to John Hamilton Reynolds," had spoken of the disillusionment that comes from seeing "Too far into the sea, where every maw/The greater on the lesser feeds evermore." Keats also spoke of "an eternal fierce destruction" at nature's center (ST, p. 214). Here, urges Eiseley, was a clear intuition of evolution.

Eiseley goes on to ponder the strong intellectual affinities between Emerson and Darwin. Radically different though these men were, they both grasped a universe in process—a prodigal, wasteful, infinitely fertile nature in whose scheme man holds no inherent preeminence (ST, p. 216). Emerson possessed a vivid sense of time's linearity, directionality, and subservience to entropy. This great transcendentalist marveled at how all animal life has contibuted "to leave the print of its features and form in someone or other of these upright heaven-facing speakers" (ST, p. 216). Unencumbered with the demands of scientific method, Emerson could give free reign to his expansive, image-making, synthetic powers. So liberated, he furnished the literate world with suggestive metaphors and rich, emotionally gripping conceptualizations; these could lure more logical minds in remarkable new directions. There is a concentrated power of image and emotion in Emerson that makes him a necessary complement to Darwin. Emerson's expansiveness allows us, avers Eiseley, to grasp the full implications of the necessarily understated hypotheses of science.

So the literary naturalists and nature poets have an indispensible role to play in the scientific enterprise. Keenly observant, attuned to deeper resonances, capable of adopting startlingly novel perspectives on their subject, intuitive, metaphorical—the greatest of them invent elegant and powerful worlds. These literary environments can nourish, stimulate and inspire good scientific work. Eiseley believed that speculative and fantasy writing served the same function (ST, p. 269). A devotee of Tolkien, Ray Bradbury, Don Stuart, and Jules Verne,

Eiseley was at work on a science-fiction novel at the time of his death (ST, p. 12). To his way of thinking this was no betrayal of his vocation. For, as he asserted in "The Illusion of Two Cultures,"

it is the successful analogy or symbol which frequently allows the scientist to leap from a generalization in one field of thought to a triumphant achievement in another. . . . Such analogies genuinely resemble the figures and enchantments of great literature, whose meanings similarly can never be totally grasped because of their endless power to ramify in the individual mind. [ST, p. 274]

Our great concern, he advised, must be to educate creative minds without regard to the disciplines they seek to enrich. Narrow professionalism, an excessive attention to concentrated specialization, the cultivation of "crystalline and icy objectivity"—these aspects of modern life infuriated Eiseley (ST, p. 276). He was particularly upset to see this same "puritanism of the spirit" invade the humanities.

8

Science and Will: On Loving the Failures of the World

Near the middle of the last century, Søren Kierkegaard protested vehemently against system building in European philosophy. Kierkegaard's main target was Hegel's *Phenomenology of Mind*. That imposing book traced the entire development of human consciousness—which, in Hegel's view, is only a partial manifestation of the mind of a world spirit. Historical epochs are the means, as it were, for the world spirit to achieve self-awareness. Although the *Phenomenology* appeared in 1807, it contained clear anticipations of evolutionary ideas. Hegel's focus was not on organic but rather on cultural and spiritual evolution. Further, the work claimed to encompass all scientific knowledge. (Hegel's dissertation had dealt with planetary orbits, and he continued to write on such purely scientific matters as electricity and heat.) Thus, when Kierkegaard lashed out at Hegel, he was attacking not only the reigning philosophy of the age but also the scientific and evolutionary habit of mind that Hegel claimed to embody.

Kierkegaard protested in the name of the real, existing individual. Oppressed by Hegel's fascination for huge and abstract processes, Kierkegaard denied that persons must be seen essentially as representatives of the forces shaping their age. The reality of individual experience and choice should, he insisted, take center stage in philosophy. Whatever the great historical tendencies that carry us along, the solitary self remains responsible and primary. In a famous image, Kierkegaard pictured Hegel as having constructed a massive structure of thought and then lived outside it in a doghouse. The point is that Hegel's system defined a reality in which Hegel himself was not personally implicated. For Kierkegaard, truth is inherently subjective; it can never emerge from an aloof, impersonal, "objective" observer who remains uninvolved in his or her own conclusions.

We do not mention Kierkegaard merely because Loren Eiseley was fond of quoting the "gloomy Dane." Rather, Kierkegaard's lonely battle sheds a clear light on some of Eiseley's most difficult essays, especially "The Star Thrower." Like Kierkegaard, Eiseley demanded to know the inner, personal meaning of great intellectual schemes. What Hegelian thought was to Kierkegaard, Darwinian evolution was to Eiseley. Both men ask the question, Where shall *I* live in this embracing system? Both conclude that if they cannot find a dwelling place within the system, then the system must be adjusted. Both rage against the cult of objectivity and reveal, through confessional forms of writing, how the soul makes its claims on the mind. Unlike Kierkegaard, Eiseley did not fashion a new perspective outside the structure of evolutionary theory. Rather, he used evolution—stretching himself toward it, letting it shape his personality, and, where it proved too confining, going beyond it.

E. Fred Carlisle has written perceptively on this part of Eiseley's artistic legacy. He emphasizes Eiseley's affinities not with Kierkegaard but with Herman Melville, whom Eiseley also greatly admired. In *Moby Dick*, Ishmael first tries to get at the mystery of the white whale through the science of taxonomy. He heaps up fact after fact about whales; he measures, dissects, classifies, compares, and analyzes. The limits of this method are reached, however, and still Moby Dick remains sovereignly unknown, uncomprehended in his full individuality. Melville urges that imagination, intuition, and the whole passionate selfhood of the viewer be brought to bear on the problem. But even this is not enough. The quest, to be successful, must risk the observer's life: "No. Only in the heart of the quickest perils; only when within the eddyings of his angry flukes; only in the profound un- bounded sea, can the fully investigated whole be truly and livingly found out."[1]

Like Kierkegaard, Melville depicts the journeying of a vulnerable, open human self toward knowledge in the fullest sense of the term. This is also the way of Eiseley's science. "For him," says Carlisle, "science is a personal quest that recognizes the self as the origin of all knowledge—even of scientific knowledge—but that also requires the systematic structure of science for its suc- cess."[2] Eiseley was fond of the idea that the true value of science lies not in what it makes of the world, but what it makes of the knower. He thus concerned himself as scientist with dread, love, despair, failure, doubt. It is not that Eiseley subjected these matters to scientific method, watching their behavior from a safe distance. That strategy would resemble Hegel's—living outside the system one discovers. Rather, Eiseley passionately dwells in the truths of science, and when these constrain him too severely, he uses them as tools for expansive speculation. Carlisle says of Eiseley, "In his writing the systematic activity and structure of science merge with the search for the self within that structure."[3] Eiseley "tries to extend science so that it comprehends more, but he is also trying to understand for himself."[4]

"The Star Thrower"

Eiseley's most powerful and complex essay, "The Star Thrower," confronts the problem of scientific knowledge and authentic selfhood. As usual, his argument is entan- gled in a dense web of narration and symbolism. The setting is Costabel, an unidentified beach rimming an unidentified sea. "Certain coasts are set aside for ship-wreck," Eiseley recalls, and Costabel is such a coast. The wreck is Eiseley himself, who has fled in despair to this place. He is borne down by a dry emptiness, a massive sense of futility, a foretaste of annihilation, an unac-countable bitterness. Eiseley attributes his mood to sci-ence, whose merciless objective gaze naturalizes and disenchants the world.

> *Who is the man walking in the Way?*
> *An eye glaring in the skull.*

These curious lines from a Buddhist sage provide Eiseley with his guiding symbol. "I was the skull," he confesses, "the inhumanly stripped skeleton without voice," pitiless, hopeless, adrift:

There was, in this desiccated skull, only an eye like a pharos light, a beacon, a search beam revolving endlessly in sunless noonday or black night. Ideas like swarms of insects rose to the beam, but the light consumed them. Upon that shore meaning had ceased. There were only the dead skull and the revolving eye. [UU, pp. 67–68]

Thus burdened, Eiseley roams the beaches of Costabel. His inner scanning picks up only death signals. The fu-rious surf casts up a multitude of sea life. Abandoned high on the sand are crabs, octopi, long-limbed starfish, shell inhabitants of every description. Those that can battle into the water are hurled back, become sand fouled, and feel their mucilaginous bodies shrivel under the rising sun. "The seabeach and its endless war are soundless," intones the narrator. "Nothing screams but the gulls" (UU, p. 69).

Afflicted with insomnia, Eiseley rises before dawn to watch a strange ritual. A storm has pounded the coast,

and, anticipating rich harvests, the shell hunters with
their flashlights have taken to the beach. In the half dark
Eiseley watches the "vulturine" activity. "A kind of greedy
madness sweeps over the competing collectors," he observes. Working with "vulgar little spades and the stick-
length pincers that eased their elderly backs," they scoop
up living specimens, favoring starfish. Then, laboring
under huge bags, they take them back to outdoor kettles
where they boil alive "the beautiful voiceless things" (UU,
p. 73).

Far up the beach, Eiseley discerns an even odder
spectacle. A great rainbow "of incredible perfection" looms
up, and beneath it a human figure can be seen flinging
objects into the breaking surf. Coming closer Eiseley
finds the man to be a different sort of collector. He gathers starfish in order to pitch them back beyond the risen
surf where they may possibly live. "The stars throw
well," observes the man. "One can help them." His
bronzed, worn face still reflects the colors of the receding
rainbow. In his eye, "a faint question" kindles, to which
Eiseley at last responds.

"I do not collect," I said uncomfortably, the wind beating at
my garments. "Neither the living nor the dead. Death is the
only successful collector." I could feel the full night blackness
in my skull and the terrible eye resuming its indifferent journey.
[UU, p. 72]

Eiseley returns to his room, beset with images of deserts,
an abyss, a rotating eye, and the star thrower.

In most of Eiseley's writing evolutionary processes
are viewed highly positively. The Darwinians discovered
a fabulous creativity pressing forth in all parts of nature.
Seemingly static worlds are revealed to be part of a moving, unexpected universe. Life is historical and therefore
inherently dramatic. But, as Darwin himself knew, a

terrifying message awaited his readers. In the middle portions of "The Star Thrower," Eiseley confronts that dark side of evolution. As he does so, we learn that his malaise is even more serious than he first intimated. Not only has science quenched his vital subjectivity. It also shows him a universe in which individuality itself is of no consequence. Worse still, at the moment that science reveals the total irrelevance of human selfhood, it portrays the individual as the helpless plaything of forces that render him destructive and irrational.

Eiseley's reflections turn on a distinction between two kinds of science. Although he does not use these phrases, it is clear that he is speaking of Newtonian and Darwinian types. Each yields its own fund of despair. The first offers a colorless picture of cosmic order. It hypothesizes mathematical simplicity, balanced forces, vast but triangulable space, and precise method. Under its sway, "The encrusted eye in the stone speaks to us of undeviating sunlight; the calculated elliptic of Halley's comet no longer forecasts world disaster. The planet plunges on through a chill void of star years, and there is little or nothing that remained unmeasured" (UU, p. 74). It was this science that frightened Pascal, who saw it as the dispeller of all things supernatural.

In *The Firmament of Time*, Eiseley had brooded over Pascal's notion that "There is nothing that we cannot make natural; there is nothing natural which we do not destroy" (FT, p. 159). In "The Star Thrower," this idea emerges even more strongly. The Newtonian revolution launched humanity on the project of demystifying nature. Out of this effort arose technology and the myth of progress. But Newton's science had nothing disturbing to say about man's mind. Indeed, from its vantage point, the inner world looked "secure, stable, and sunlit" (UU, p. 84). Not surprisingly, Newtonians did not perceive

that technology (and science itself) might be "linked in-
tangibly to the subconscious poltergeist aspect of man's
nature" (UU, p. 81). These sorts of insights were available only to primitive peoples, or they remained in the
locked vault of Western folklore and legend. Meanwhile,
the tools of technology became gigantic, achieving "a
revolutionary independence from their masters" (UU, p.
81). Once safe in the enchanted forest and the sacred
village, humanity now followed Newton and Bacon out
onto homeless frontiers, "the indescribable world of the
natural" (UU, p. 81).

   Darwin, and then Freud, supplied a newer and more
terrifying disenchantment. With them, "the science of
the level plains" yields to "the science of remote abysses."
Darwin "sought to visualize in a tangled bank of leaves
the silent and insatiable war of nature" (UU, p. 83).
Humanity's behavior he reduced to the same purely sel-
fish struggle that he believed is everywhere evident.
Thanks to Darwin, "the sign of the dark cave and the
club became so firmly fixed in human thinking that in
our time it has been invoked as signifying man's true
image in books selling in the hundreds of thousands"
(UU, p. 84). Freud uncovered the shape of the unconscious and "revealed it as a place of contending furies"
(UU, p. 84). Just as the evolutionists had "detected the
reptile under the lifted feathers of the bird," so Freud
had found an aggressive, animal self below the surface
provided by the ego (UU, p. 79).

   Most devastating of all, however, is modern science's
rejection of all discrete, stable individuality. Revealed to
us is a world of pure process: "Form, since the rise of
evolutionary philosophy, has itself taken on an illusory
quality," says Eiseley. "Our apparent shapes no longer
have the stability of a single divine fiat. Instead, they
waver and dissolve into the unexpected" (UU, pp. 75–

76). We learn to distrust our own experience. For we recognize ourselves as mere aspects or projections of more fundamental processes. Ultimately, we are mere containers of life; only *its* reality is the truly real. The science of remote abysses "no longer shelters man." Instead "it reveals him in vaporous metamorphic succession as the unspecified one, the creature of the magic flight" (UU, p. 80).

"Death is the only successful collector." The full significance of Eiseley's earlier remark now becomes apparent. In the struggle on the beach, the star thrower ignorantly set himself in opposition to the entire inclination of the universe. The cookers of starfish recognize that their victims have lost. The war goes on at all levels in nature, they reason wisely, and there is no point in worrying about the losers.

The narrative is resumed. "All this devious, tattered way was exposed to the ceaseless turning eye within the skull that lay hidden on the bed in Costabel" (UU, p. 79). Gradually, Eiseley senses the presence of another eye, its origin unclear, emerging from memory. He finally identifies it as an eye torn from a photograph. Against his will, he faces the knowledge that the eye belongs to his mother. The ruminations start up again, then fade out completely. Eiseley remembers an attic where he found the few things his mother bequeathed him. He comes upon an old packet of family portrait photos dating from the 1880s. In one of them his mother, then six years old, appears. Even then, Eiseley knows, she had been losing her hearing. "The eyes in the photograph were already remote and shadowed by some inner turmoil. The poise of the body was already that of one miserably departing the peripheries of the human estate" (UU, pp. 85–86). Her life as a deaf, "ill-taught prairie artist" had been punctuated with mental breakdown. Although dead, she now imposes herself on Eiseley's consciousness, demanding that he come to terms with her reality.

In the darkness of the room, he puts on sunglasses. The revolving beam in his mind has stopped. At last, there is "an utter stillness, a waiting for a cosmic judgment." A Biblical injunction crosses his mind: "Love not the world, neither the things that are in the world." The torn eye, his mother's, considers him.

"But I *do* love the world," I whispered to a waiting presence in the empty room. "I love its small ones, the things beaten in the strangling surf, the bird, singing, which flies and falls and is not seen again." I choked and said, with the torn eye still upon me. "I love the lost ones, the failures of the world." [UU, p. 86]

This confession uttered, Eiseley, like the Ancient Mariner, finds his great burden being lifted. Drawn from him finally in this soft-spoken climactic moment has been an admission of love for his own mother. Bitter and troubled memories of her had long plagued him, as Eiseley's autobiography makes clear. So this acknowledgement seems almost to come as a surprise to him. Her ghost is freed. "The torn eye," he reports, "surveyed me sadly and was gone."

But to step across the rift that separates him from his mother is, Eiseley realized, to bind himself irrevokably to the unsuccessful in nature. Deaf and half-crazed, Daisy Corey Eiseley epitomized all "the lost ones." In embracing her, choosing to acknowledge himself as her son, Eiseley also faces up to what is lost and failed in his own life. Of the experience he says, "It was like the renunciation of my scientific heritage." That heritage enshrines only those starfish who evade "the strangling surf." It predicts the vicious dawn labors of the shell collectors. It cannot comprehend a creature who refuses to compete, or who, against the tide, freely chooses not only to be merciful to the failures but to identify with them. Between the successful and the unsuccessful lies a great rift. Can a creature "born of Darwinian struggle, in the silent war under the tangled bank" be expected to cross that rift? "No," answers the determinist voice of science. "Yes," replies one who has experienced "the awesome freedom to choose"—to choose "beyond the narrowly circumscribed circle that delimits the animal being" (UU, p. 88).

The essay concludes with Eiseley's reunion on the beach with the star thrower. Under Eiseley's artistic control, the scene becomes a celebration of "the human right to define his own frontier," to contravene the ways of nature as described by the withering eye of professional science (UU, p. 87). Together, Eiseley and his colleague spin the living starfish far out beyond the danger point. The eye they see with is an inward eye, an eye "not under the restraints to be apprehended from what is vulgarly called the natural" (UU, p. 88). They are throwers who love "not man, but life" (UU, p. 91). This inner liberty is part of what Eiseley meant by the second world, and he recalls again Bacon's plea that science be employed "for the uses of life" (UU, p. 91). His encounter with the star thrower has made it clear that in science itself there is no power to choose that usage. The choice, if it is made at all, will come from a solitary self whose choosing act defines a world beyond nature.

God and the Reconciliation of the Species

"The Star Thrower" may well be an existentialist classic, inviting comparison with the efforts of Kierkegaard, Sartre, or Camus. But to associate Eiseley with these writers forces one to pose to him the great question each addressed: does an individual who risks all in a self-defining, self-determined choice come into alignment with some fundamental tendency in things? Or, is the action absurd, as absurd indeed as the universe itself? If the whole body of Eiseley writings is taken as evidence, then he must be ranked with the likes of Camus, to whom the universe seemed benignly indifferent to the human drama. Eiseley persistently pictures the immense journey of human consciousness as a lonely affair played out in an alien universe. If, however, "The Star Thrower" and a few other essays become authoritative, then Eiseley stands with Kierkegaard and the other theistic existentialists. Indeed, it is not difficult to see "The Star Thrower" as a specifically Christian affirmation.

The Christianity of "The Star Thrower" is mystical. Emerson and Meister Eckhart inspire its ecstatic conclusion as well as its symbols. By the end of the essay, the rainbow, the eye, and star thrower all have become emblems of divinity. In the Old Testament, of course, the rainbow is the sign of God's covenant with the earth. It appears after Noah's ordeal is over as God's promise to "every creature of all flesh" never to destroy life by the waters of the flood. Read metaphorically, this text asserts God's intention to restrain the violence of nature out of concern for his fleshly creation. This ancient meaning gives resonance to Eiseley's use of the rainbow as a sign of compassion, perfection, and the ecologic unity of nature. As he hurls starfish, he reflects that some individuals have always cherished "the memory of the perfect circle of compassion from life to death and back to life— the completion of the rainbow of existence" (UU, p. 90).

"The eye with which I see God is the same as that with which he sees me." Meister Eckhart, the German mystic, uttered this aphorism in the early fourteenth cen-

tury. Ralph Waldo Emerson, the American transcendentalist, wrote: "Standing on bare ground, my head
bathed by the blithe air and uplifted into infinite space,
all mean egotism vanishes. I become a transparent eye-
ball; I am nothing, I see all; the currents of the Universal
Being circulate through me; I am part or parcel of God"
(quoted in ST, p. 211). Eiseley meant his own meditations to build on the imaginative work of these two great
souls. In its final mutation, his controlling symbol assumes a pantheistic character.

Out of the depths of a seemingly empty universe had grown
an eye, like the eye in my room, but an eye on a vastly larger
scale. It looked out upon what I can only call itself. It searched
the skies and it searched the depths of being. In the shape of
man it had ascended like a vaporous emanation from the depths
of night. The nothing had miraculously gazed upon the nothing
and was not content. It was an intrusion into, or a projection
out of, nature for which no precedent existed. The act was, in
short, an assertion of value arisen from the domain of absolute
zero. A little whirlwind of commingling molecules had succeeded in confronting its own universe. [UU, p. 87]

A pure pantheist would rest the matter here. Although the essay does go on to speak of "some ancient,
inexhaustible, and patient intelligence" gathering itself
into a universe, Eiseley leaves the reader with the sense
that this Otherness has a personal dimension. After his
first exchange with the star thrower, Eiseley remarked
that "He had, at any rate, the posture of a god." In his
final appearance, the figure and his gestures are a complex
image of God and his relation to the world. Working
beside the unspeaking Sisyphus at water's edge, Eiseley
senses that they are imitating a greater, more profound
motion. As the starfish are sown beyond "the insatiable
waters of death" (UU, p. 90),

somewhere far off, across bottomless abysses, I felt as though another world was flung more joyfully. I could have thrown in a frenzy of joy, but I set my shoulders and cast, as the thrower in the rainbow cast, slowly, deliberately, and well. The task was not to be assumed lightly, for it was men as well as starfish that we sought to save. For a moment, we cast on an infinite beach together beside an unknown hurler of suns. [UU, p. 90]

The theological ideas present here are startling. The hidden God who creates the unimaginable gigantic and unfathomable worlds of nature also is the God of "the lost ones." Indeed, the rescue of these failures is achieved with the same motion that creates this universe. The thrower "loves not man but life"; nevertheless, humanity plays a special role in his scheme. Through humanity, the "tangled bank of unceasing struggle, selfishness, and death" is discovered in all its hideousness (UU, p. 91). But with humanity's emergence, there also arises the freedom to ignore the struggle and "madly" assert love for the competitor. To choose the way of love requires a risk, the pains of which no science can ease. But if taken, the risk leads to the discovery of a deity also freely embarked on a vast project of reconciliation. Humans are invited to be star throwers, cooperators in a stupendous and perhaps impossible venture. At the same time, they themselves are doomed starfish, rescued by a hurler of stars who walks "because he chooses, always in desolation, but not in defeat" (UU, p. 91).

The star thrower on the beach is thus an image of both God and Christ—albeit a novel and disturbing image. Merely mortal, subjected to the same realities of competition and struggle that victimize the starfish, setting himself against the grain of the natural, he gives himself in faith to these castoffs. The traditional Christ symbols of fish, sea, star, and cross resonate delicately in the background of the essay, but Eiseley has forged them into a new, biocentric shape. For the star thrower identifies himself not only with humans but also (and perhaps more so) with the lower organisms he is saving. He is the messiah of all creation, the consolation for the cruelties of evolution. Once again the intensely Franciscan character of Eiseley's Christianity is evident.

"The Star Thrower" is by no means Eiseley's only theological essay nor the only evidence of his essentially Christian mysticism. "The Lethal Factor" (ST) concluded with a confession of faith in "that lost receding figure on the dreadful hill of Calvary" (ST, p. 266). "The Chresmologue" (NC) seems to be a call for a return to the revolutionary inwardness of Christ; significantly, Eiseley draws inspiration from the anonymous author of the Christian mystical classic, *The Cloud of Unknowing*. "How Natural is 'Natural'?" (FT and ST) invokes Pascal, Kierkegaard, and John Donne, as Eiseley again struggles to reconcile contending species and achieve union with "the world beyond the nature that we know" (FT, p. 179). Examples can be multiplied. Over a score of star-throwing acts—gestures that make nature more of a peaceable kingdom—appear in the essays and poetry.

9

Eiseley Unleashed: Ventures in Surrealism

To the public, Loren Eiseley cultivated an image of dignified propriety, moral seriousness, and professionalism. His well-chosen suits and grave, courteous bearing projected correctness. His rugged, handsome face expressed colossal reserve, and a definite majesty was added by his deep, well-modulated speaking voice. Documentary and educational filmmakers clamored for his services as narrator and commentator. To decades of graduating classes he was the epitome of humanistic science.

But as we have already seen, there was the "night country" Eiseley—a denizen of "all the strange hours," a nature mystic capable of proclaiming: "I, the professor, trembling absurdly on the platform with my book and my spectacles, am the single philosophical animal. I am the unfolding worm, and mud fish, the weird tree of Igdrasil shaping itself endlessly out of darkness towards the light" (FT, p. 168). Insomniac, haunter of all-night restaurants, frequenter of junkyards and burning trash dumps, this other Eiseley was given to fingering the hair of dead dogs or studying a giant slug "feeding from a runnel of pink ice-cream in an abandoned Dixie cup" (NC, p. 229).

While we have revealed some of Eiseley's night-stalking side, our focus on the interrelation of his key themes has perhaps held him too much in the daylight. It will be fitting, then, to include a few final glimpses of that remarkable twilight world that Eiseley, unleashed by the potent agency of insomnia, discovered and explored. It is, most assuredly, a surreal world, a domain wherein the vivid illogic of nightmares and semiconscious musings reassembles things and connections. It is a realm from which the "fact-value dichotomy" has been banished; and therefore moral and aesthetic relations immediately and simultaneously become physical relations.

It is, in short, a place for perceiving the noumena within the phenomena.

Eiseley's night country is not entirely the same superreal terrain marked out by André Breton in his famous 1924 surrealist manifesto, however. There Breton indicated that the surrealist style was based on "psychic automatism in its pure state, by which one proposes to express—verbally...—the actual functioning of thought...in the absence of any control exercised by reason, exempt from any aesthetic or moral concern."[1] Eiseley's surrealist ventures have a controlled feel about them. They strike one as somehow disciplined or at least partly deliberate. "Pure automatism" is not a phrase one wants to associate with them. Eiseley's encounters with the fantastic and the surreal were, we believe, controlled experiments that fit into his life-long project of finding personal significance in a world framed by impersonal scientific laws.

The surrealist tendencies in "The Dance of the Frogs" (ST), and "The Creature from the Marsh" (NC) have already been remarked. But in a host of other writings Eiseley produces literary near-equivalents of paintings by Dali, Man Ray, or Tanguy. "How Natural is 'Natural'?" (FT and ST) describes Eiseley mounting the lecturer's rostrum to address a college class. The subject is evolution, and as he talks and writes on the blackboard he wonders how the students can possibly enter his time-obsessed mental reality. There is a question from the back: "Doctor, do you believe there is a direction to evolution?" Eiseley reports, "Instead of the words, I hear a faint piping, and see an eager scholar's face squeezing and dissolving on the body of a chest-thumping ape" (FT, p. 168). The question is repeated.

I see it then—the trunk that stretches monstrously behind him.
It winds out of the door, down dark and obscure corridors to
the cellar, and vanishes into the floor. It writhes, it crawls, it
barks and snuffles and roars, and the odor of the swamp exhales
from it. That pale young scholar's face is the last bloom on a
curious animal extrusion through time. . . . I too am a many-
visaged thing that has climbed upward out of the dark of endless
leaf falls, and has slunk, furred, through the glitter of blue
glacial nights. [FT, p. 168]

Like all surrealists, Eiseley affirms that this vision "is not
an illusion" (FT, p. 168). The fecundity of the human
brain is inexhaustible, he notes, but few people take the
time to plant the seeds of contemplation.

Eiseley's mysticism draws sustenance from his surrealist inclinations. This fact is most evident in "One
Night's Dying," a short meditational piece so perfect in
execution that one might read it a dozen times and still
discover new things. Its subject is insomnia. Through a
series of anecdotes, remembrances, and observations,
Eiseley develops the idea that while nothing is worse than
chronic sleeplessness, the insomniac is often rewarded
with unusual insights and visions. "It is the sufferer from
insomnia," he writes, "who knits the torn edges of men's
dreams together in the hour before dawn" (NC, p. 176).
This idea is the meditational fulcrum of the essay.

He includes a scene worthy of Federico Fellini.
Walking sleepless at dawn in Manhattan, he ruminates
on the long history of *Columbia livia*, the common pigeon.
The bird, he sees, "has been with us since our beginning
and has adapted as readily as ourselves to the artificial
cliffs of man's first cities" (NC, p. 174). Then, just as he
is preoccupied with the fate of one particular injured
pigeon stranded on a street corner, Eiseley half hears the
"dreadful robot rhythm" of New Yorkers on their way

to work. Suddenly a tide of human machines carries him off and deposits him a block away. "My bird," he reports, "had vanished under that crunching, multifooted current as remorselessly as the wounded duck under the indifferent combers of the sea" (NC, p. 175). He experiences himself as an "unwilling droplet" in this human ocean— this mechanical sea that marches, ruthless, towards death. "I have never returned to search in that particular street for the face of humanity," he concludes. "I prefer the endlessly rolling pebbles of the tide, the moonstones polished by the pulling moon" (NC, p. 176).

The essay's main episode finds Eiseley stranded in a foreign airport. A night-long ordeal of waiting continues; for, having missed his plane, he must spend endless hours under the sleep-cancelling glare of the efficient terminal lights. His vexation, exhaustion, and loneliness mount. The slightest additional effort seems completely unbearable. Later, his throbbing head rested on a hand, Eiseley observes a man coming very slowly toward him with grotesque, limping movements. He dismisses the image. But after a time he feels the pain-ridden body approaching closer. The anatomist in Eiseley suddenly takes over and he sees the figure as an "amazing conglomeration of sticks and broken, misshapen pulleys." The utter inadequacy of the human body comes home to him: "How could anyone, I contended, trapped in this mechanical thing of joints and sliding wires expect the acts it performed to go other than awry?" (NC, p. 177).

As the man limps on relentlessly, Eiseley upbraids God and curses the grossness of mortal substance. "How for a single minute," he asks, "could we dream or imagine that thought would save us, children deliver us, from the body of this death?" The old man, "breathing heavily, lunging and shuffling upon his cane," is now upon Eiseley (NC, p. 177).

And then this strange thing happened, which I do not mean physically and cannot explain. The man entered me. From that moment I saw him no more. For a moment I was contorted within his shape, and then out of his body—our bodies, rather—there arose some inexplicable sweetness of union, some understanding between spirit and body which I had never before experienced. Was it I, the joints and pulleys only, who desired this peace so much? [NC, pp. 177–178]

As he gathers up his luggage to board his plane, Eiseley feels himself limping with growing age. "Something of that terrible passer lingered in my bones," he says, "yet I was released, the very room had dilated." A fragment of scripture comes to his lips: "Beareth all things." The words come from St. Paul; earlier in the essay they had appeared in fuller form: "Beareth all things, believeth all things, hopeth all things, endureth all things." Eiseley never speaks directly of the subject of Paul's sentence. Somehow the essay does not need to mention it.

Other instances of Eiseley's fascination for surrealist ventures come quickly to mind. The second part of "Science and the Sense of the Holy" begins with a lucid commentary on a surrealist painting by the contemporary artist Irwin Fleminger. Entitled "Laws of Nature," the work gave Eiseley a graphic confirmation of his feeling that outside the reach of the so-called order imposed by human reason is something gigantic, too great, certainly not bound by human powers (ST, p. 192). Of the painting he wrote, "Here in a jumbled desert waste without visible life two thin laths had been erected a little distance apart. Strung across the top of the laths was an insubstantial string with even more insubstantial filaments depending from the connecting cord" (ST, p. 192). The effect, he attests, was terrifying. Vast, ominous, complex areas lay outside the puny reach of humanity. Our vaunted natural law—"so much dangling string and frail slats"—

"would not have sufficed to fence a chicken run" (ST, p. 192).

For Loren Eiseley, surrealist vision is not an end in itself. His discovery of a moral in Fleminger's painting betrays his reluctance to let the work stand on its own, uninterpreted. Indulgence in pure, unguided fantasy is not Eiseley's way. Rather, surrealism is an exercise in inner seeing, another way of opening up the inner galaxy. His surrealistic ventures thus stand alongside his mnemonic attempts to recover not only his personal past but also that of the species. One must always bear in mind that Eiseley came very close to abolishing the distinction between inner and outer realities. So his surrealist moments merge with his quest for the miraculous outside of science.

This merging is evident in a major essay, "The Innocent Fox." Were one to choose an accompanying illustration for it, Fleminger's painting might serve. Eiseley wishes to show how an encounter with the wild reality lying beyond our natural laws can renew a sense of wonder. Through a series of narratives he tries to help us find "the hole in the hedge leading to the unforeseen" (UU, p. 196). Before commencing these, he reminds his reader that although we imagine we are day creatures "we grope in a lawless and smoky realm toward an exit that eludes us" (UU, p. 195). Yet we know "that such an exit exists."

A sequence of miracles and reflections on the nature of the miraculous constitutes "The Innocent Fox." Eiseley is in a dry period; he wants to banish the old fear that miracles never happen. Prowling in his study at midnight, he surveys the neighboring housetops for something interesting. He is startled to see in a high dormer window of a nearby Victorian house a giant bolt of lightning playing forth from a great condenser. Each succeeding night, at the same dead hour, the blue bolt leaps in the attic room. "I dreamed, staring from my window, of that coruscating arc revivifying flesh or leaping sentient beyond it into some unguessed state of being" (UU, p. 199). The event captivates him. He imagines absorbed youthful scientists opening wholly new vistas in science. His own dreams of doing great experimental work are rekindled. But the nocturnal researches end; autumn passes, and Eiseley is left with his disappointment.

But he now knows that the miracle he seeks must be "elsewhere than in retorts or coiled wire" (UU, p. 200). The laboratory under the cupola comes to signify for him the ersatz prodigies of science. Impressive as its achievements are, they appeal mainly to our outer eye, engaging our lust for the immediately spectacular. Something far more subjective and more connected with "the animal aspect of things," he decides, is what the wise miracle seeker must have. Eiseley thus quests inward, outside of science, as he did in "The Star Thrower."

Eiseley then relates a night automobile drive through pine mountains. For hours he twists down rutted roads, concentrating on the demanding task. Intense weariness besets him, but he drives on. It then occurs to him that just beyond the reach of his headlights an amazingly fleet creature is keeping pace with his car. He can't make out its dimensions, color, or species: "Sometimes it seemed to be bounding forward. Sometimes it seemed to present a face to me and dance backward" (UU, p. 202). He wonders if it is an animal at all. Momentarily, the form becomes the floating head commemorated in Iroquois masks. Then Eiseley thinks of a windigo, the cannibal demon of Ojibwa legend. He feels his own blood—not urban, almost not human, "from other times and a far place"

—rising in response to the shape-shifting beast (UU, p. 202).

Eiseley finally discovers that "the creature who had assigned himself to me was an absurdly spotted dog of dubious affinities" (UU, p. 203). But this neither disappoints nor relieves him. For the apparition has somehow launched Eiseley into a new perceptual framework. He has glimpsed Fleminger's "far wilder and more formidable" order (UU, p. 202) lurking beyond the realm of natural law. He understands all too clearly the artificiality of human mental constructs. Our consciousness, he realizes, insists on taming, domesticating, and shrinking its perceptions to its own size. Unable to force the gigantic leapings and glidings of nonhuman reality, it transforms them into spotted dogs.

Language tricks us into thinking that "our self-drawn categories" really exist in "the inhuman, unpopulated wood" (UU, p. 203). But they don't. We must confess, argues Eiseley, that the succession of forms momentarily frozen into the shape "dog" may not remain such when our backs are turned. After all, that which was identified so confidently "had been picked by me out of a running weave of colors and faces into which it would lapse once more." But if this is true of the dog, it applies also to the human interpreter of the dog. It too is but the creation of "a nerve net and the lens of an eye":

Like the dog, I was destined to leap away at last into the unknown wood. My flesh, my own seeming unique individuality, was already slipping like flying mist, like the colors of the dog, away from the little parcel of my bones. [UU, p. 203]

Thus the definiteness we feel ourself to possess is a comforting illusion, says Eiseley. Such surreal experiences are necessary to jar open the doors of perception.

Miracle is a matter of philosophic seeing. It is an aware-
ness of the vast spaces between subatomic particles and
the lurking potentiality of evolutionary change. Our
problem, Eiseley insists, is excessive concentration on
the given. We must go beyond science when science
becomes obsessed with manipulating the external world.
Too much measuring of empirical reality causes us to
forget that, as the epigraph for "The Innocent Fox" states,
"all things are crouched in eagerness to become something
else" (UU, p. 194). This applies to things both mental
and physical. And Eiseley, by means of his surrealistic
experiments, demonstrates the invalidity of this distinction.

The final section of "The Innocent Fox," like its
companion essay, "The Last Neanderthal," explores what
for Eiseley is the greatest miracle of all, human memory.
It is a delicate and haunting piece of writing. Imitating
the free, enchanting play of remembrance, Eiseley finally
brings us to his father's deathbed. He sees himself as his
father's memory. He sees, as through his father's eyes,
the dying body. Yet the hands remain curiously respon-
sive. After forty years of pondering the scene, Eiseley
now understands the question his father was silently asking: "Why are you, my hands, so separate from me at
death, yet still to be commanded?" The great massive
otherness of the body, the mystery of our command over
it as well as its independent power, the way the self is a
dispersible center in the nexus of flesh—all this emerges
in Eiseley's reverie.

"In my beginning is my end." This is not Eiseley's
line but that of T. S. Eliot. This is the ultimate message
of "The Innocent Fox." To understand it, one must exercise not only memory but imagination. The world must
be reconstructed, says Eiseley, from ground level, from
the perspective of a playful fox cub. This delightful crea-

ture happens upon Eiseley after the writer has sojourned
the night on a desolate foggy beach. The little fox bids
him play, ignoring the niceties of evolutionary theory
and the struggle among species. The scientist finds himself on his knees, growling, with a bone in his mouth,
ecstatic at this droll adventure. The fox, he sees, is brother,
forefather, jester, and discloser of an improtant truth. It
is no longer enough to become as little children. A third,
animal eye must sprout from our foreheads so that we
no longer are "gazing with upright human arrogance upon
the things of the world" (UU, p. 209).

But remembrance too has to be cultivated so that
our points of departure are always as luminous as the
roadway itself. When Eiseley remembers himself remembering his father's death, he sees that "the meaning was
all in the beginning, as though time was awry." We store
up treasures in the only heaven available to us when we
make contact with our beginning. The universe is what
it is and what it is not. The tree we loved as children is
still growing in some dimension and certainly in our
memory. The selves we have rejected enjoy a career elsewhere, but we know them in memory. "If I were to
render a report on this episode," concludes Eiseley,

I would say that men must find a way to run the arrow backward. Doubtless it is impossible in the physical world, but in
the memory and the will man might achieve the deed if he
would try. [UU, p. 211]

From this brief account of some of Eiseley's surrealist ventures, it seems clear that pure psychic automatism is not exactly what Eiseley is about. There are rational
and moral preoccupations that place a distinct pressure
on these reveries, and one must admit that there are
literary preoccupations as well. "One Night's Dying" is
both a free-floating experience report and a covert lesson

on Christian love. "The Innocent Fox" is both an ensem-
ble of numinous moments and a deliberate attack on em-
piricism and unidimensional habits of thought. One is
reminded of Freud's response to the work of Salvador
Dali: he found it too much mediated by theories of what
the unconscious contains. Eiseley, one might say, remained mainly on the threshhold of true surrealist release. But his art seems hardly the worse for that.

All the Strange Hours:
An
Autobiographical
Masterpiece

As the controlling epigraph for *All the Strange Hours*, Eiseley selected these lines from Robert Browning's "The Ring and the Book"——

> I' the color the tale takes, there's change perhaps
> 'Tis natural, since the sky is different,
> Eclipse in the air now, still the outline stays.[1]

Eiseley's tale is his autobiography. In his concealed essays, he had long been unfolding it. So thorough had been the self-disclosure that many of Eiseley's associates wondered what remained undivulged. Browning's words help Eiseley announce his intentions: although the tale's outline holds, a different hue casts itself over things. "Eclipse in the air" refers to impending death, the main source of the altered color scheme. *All the Strange Hours* is, says Eiseley, "the excavation of a life," a digging in the rubble of a dead personal city. Surprisingly, under that differently hued sky, things lose their usual appearance. The Eiseley unearthed in the book is both familiar and very strange.

How Eiseley renders his autobiography is nearly as revealing as what he says in it. Exceptionally well wrought, *All the Strange Hours* betrays a fierce determination on Eiseley's part to control, shape, and frame his material. (He labored on the volume for well over ten years.) There are three sections, each preceded by its own epigraph and each bearing a title: "Days of a Drifter," "Days of a Thinker," and "Days of a Doubter." Within the sections are chapters that are given such titles—in Eiseley's archly literary fashion—as "The Rat That Danced," "The Crevice and the Eye," "The Ghost World," "The Time Traders," "The Dancers in the Ring." Some of these chapters first appeared as essays in popular periodicals, and many of those that did not are sufficiently self-contained to guarantee their future inclusion in collections

140

and anthologies. Eiseley's essayistic impulse is thus manifest once again. This does not, however, make for a poorly unified book. On the contrary, though anecdotal and episodic, the chapters are bound together by a careful use of recurrent symbols, themes, and narrative patterns.

This degree of literary intentionality and control is unusual in an autobiography.[2] Although told in the first person, the tale is prepared for maximum effect, calculated and proportioned to imitate spontaneity. At times, Eiseley seems not so much to be presenting a life as creating a character. The richness and profusion of symbols is striking. Purposeful ambiguities and omissions force the reader to pause, interpret, and attend closely to descant as well as melody. Elegant, complex, lyrical, and yet powerfully dramatic, *All the Strange Hours* demands (and merits) several readings. A novelistic quality suffuses the book. Without perhaps recognizing the full significance of his own words, William Stafford remarks of *All the Strange Hours* that "all through the story the reader feels the presence of the narrator, a helpful presence, a knowing presence, but also a companion for the reader's questioning and puzzlement and fear."[3] "Story," "narrator," "companion" are not terms one ordinarily uses when talking about autobiography, yet Stafford's diction is accurate. It reveals much about Eiseley's hopes for what the book could accomplish.

Eiseley's preoccupation with presence, authorial control, and formal literary effect is intimately related to that struggle against loneliness around which the book revolves. A subtitle Eiseley considered for his autobiography was "A Chronicle of Solitude." One of Eiseley's great personal achievements was to discover the uses of his loneliness, to convert it into the positive condition of solitude. But the conversion was long in coming and accompanied by much melancholy and bitterness. For as

All the Strange Hours shows, Eiseley believed that he had
been forced into unnatural, damaging isolation by his
mother's condition. As he acknowledged in "The Star
Thrower," his great burden in life was to come to terms
with his tormented mental images of her.

Chapter 3, "The Running Man," is one of several
in which Eiseley reveals various aspects of this crucial
relationship. We learn that Daisy Eiseley's roots were in
the Shepard family, noted for its tendency towards de-
mentia. As a child, Loren heard "the mad Shepards"
discussed in whispers. "When I was recalcitrant the Shepards were spoken of and linked with my name," he
recalls (ASH, p. 25). One must bear in mind that prior
to the first world war, American society displayed little
tolerance for mental illness. In the small-town midwest,
"madness" and "breakdown" were blights on family honor,
feared signs of congenital weakness, dreaded sources of
public shame. Thus, when the deaf woman slipped into
instability, her husband made sure she was isolated from
as many people as possible. He instructed Loren, "Your
mother is not responsible, son. Do not cross her" (ASH,
p. 30).

Out of love and respect for his father, says Eiseley,
he obeyed as best he could. But not crossing the "hys-
terical" and obsessed woman meant that the boy had to
give up close friendships and indeed renounce most normal social relationships. He tells of playing one day with
some schoolmates in the fields around Aurora, Nebraska.
Restless, possessive, and disagreeable, Daisy Eiseley
"pursued us to a nearby pasture and in the rasping voice
of deafness ordered me home." His standing in his beloved gang was suddenly at stake. The cruelty and arbitrariness of the woman utterly humiliated him. "My
mother," he wrote, "was behaving in the manner of a
witch. She could not hear, she was violently gesticulating

without dignity, and her dress was somehow appropriate to the occasion" (ASH, p. 32). He disobeyed her and ran away with his chuckling friends, "the witch, her hair flying, her clothing disarrayed, stumbling after" (ASH, p. 32). Later his shame knew no bounds. He had violated the promise to his father, advertised his family's ignominy to the neighborhood, and hurt his mother.

Eiseley believes that this family dilemma deeply scarred his psyche. Essentially an only child, his father away most of the time, cut off from his mother by her deafness, he achingly yearned to belong to his gang. But when he succeeded in friendship, his mother jealously severed the bonds. To thwart her would be to injure an innocent woman and show ingratitude to his father. (That his father did not follow the advice of relatives to desert the family made a great impression on the boy.) When Eiseley later married, he decided against children because he feared the effects of "Shepard blood." His mother's condition forced him back on himself at every point. He could enjoy the fullness of human society only at the price of her discomfort which in turn would bring pain to his father. Thus, Eiseley's hatred for her was always translated into self-hatred. About the incident in the fields Eiseley says, "Only an unutterable savagery, my savagery at myself, scrawls it once and once only for this page" (ASH, p. 32).

Eiseley traces his own inner restlessness, his lonely venturing, to these early experiences. He acknowledges a penchant for flight, escape, running born in boyhood moments of fleeing his mother. "Even today, as though in a far-off crystal, I can see my running, gesticulating mother and her distorted features cursing us" (ASH, p. 32). In desperate need of being drawn lovingly to her, he instead felt compelled to desert. A deep pattern of drifting and detachment was established in his character—a profound, urgent desire to belong, coupled with an inability to cement deep human union. The fellowships he later treasured were mostly temporary ones: brother rail riders during the Depression; a group of drifters stranded at a Kansas whistle stop; an itinerant chauffeur in California; bone hunters on a summer dig; a huge-handed merchant seaman met on a New York train; foreign students in Philadelphia. The word "stranger" came to have highly charged significance for him. Significantly, Frank Speck, his great friend and mentor at the University of Pennsylvania, "was basically as alone as myself" (ASH, p. 124). Of Eiseley's autobiographical writings W. H. Auden perceptively observed:

> After reading them, I get the impression of a wanderer who is often in danger of being shipwrecked on the shores of Dejection . . . and a solitary who feels more easily at home with animals than with his fellow human beings. Aside from figures in his childhood, the human beings who have "messages" for him are all total strangers.[4]

Eiseley's failure to belong—to embrace an enduring and sustaining human community—helps explain his avidity for literary form. The discipline and inner control he might have received from true fellowship had to be self-imposed. Eiseley reached out for whatever sources of discipline were available to him, including the discipline of literature. His preoccupation with verbal structures was part of his larger quest for a communal order in which he could settle and define his own selfhood.*

---

*It is significant that Eiseley possessed a highly developed sense of audience. He had an unerring eye for what was appropriate and fitting for the particular group he was addressing. To a great extent he allowed the expectations and needs of his

His need for such controls was very great. His romantic expansiveness was paralleled by a volcanic temper that Eiseley had constantly to guard against. In *All the Strange Hours* he speaks about "his split personality"—the scholarly, meditational self and "the murderer who had not murdered" (ASH, p. 12). He dwells on an incident from his freight-hopping days when he came near to obeying the "pulsing red wire" in his brain by killing a brakeman. And he returns to a boyhood encounter with a neighborhood bully, when he discovered his capacity for viciousness.

> But then came the rage, the utter fury, summoned up from a thousand home repressions, adrenalin pumped into me from my Viking grandfather, the throwback from the long ships, the berserk men who cared nothing for living when the mood came on them and they stormed the English towns. It comes to me now that the Irishman must have seen it in my eyes. By nature I was a quiet reclusive boy, but then I went utterly mad. [ASH, pp. 29–30]

It seems little wonder that Eiseley's early poetry was meticulously regimented, that he suffered intense anguish after being rejected for military service, and that despite his self-description as a "fugitive" and "wanderer" he invoked his family's traditions with the dispropor-

---

audiences to dictate the method by which he would present any material. At the same time, through his most intimate writing he sought to find and shape a community that would appreciate his struggles. His popular works reached out to other lonely, diffuse souls, those who would instinctively respond to such words as: "Man is at heart a romantic." He believes in thunder, the destruction of worlds, the voice of the whirlwind" (FT, p. 3). Eiseley gradually came to have a devoted following, a loyal tribe of fans, with whom he corresponded extensively and who increasingly became the objects of his literary ventures.

tionate enthusiasm of a geneologist. When there is so much to contain and to order, the quest for form will necessarily be intense.

If *All the Strange Hours* is a chronicle of solitude, the self-disclosure of a lonely man, it also is a pilgrim's progress. Indeed, reluctant Christian that he was, Eiseley loved Bunyan's great image of a journey to the celestial city. But Eiseley was not a pilgrim who endured temptation by things that would strip him of his religious identity. Rather, he was in search of identity itself; he was a Darwinian pilgrim, too much in process to feel comfortable with any identifying guise. The autobiography is thus a record of Eiseley's experiments at self-definition. Obsessed with names, masks, and costumes, the book presents us with a sequence of discarded images of Eiseley's selfhood.

The dominant symbols of *All the Strange Hours* are concerned with identity—its elusiveness and final impossibility in an unexpected universe. The book's first sentence speaks of "a beautiful silver-backed Victorian hand mirror," one of a pair given to his aunt by Eiseley's maternal grandfather. Eiseley's mother had the other mirror, but "the last time I had seen my mother's mirror, it had been scarred by petulant violence and the handle had been snapped off." Finally, his mother's mirror disappeared, and "the face of a child vanished with it, my own face" (ASH, p. 3). In the last chapter, the mirror image returns, combining with the symbol of gambling against time.

Eiseley had earlier described a curious childhood experience of coming across his own name among some papers found in a ruined farmhouse. He had also found a pair of dice, and, as the sun set, he imitated the adults, casting dice over and over. "Then, clutching the dice, but not the paper with my name, I fled frantically down the leaf-sodden unused road, never to return" (ASH, p. 29). In his final remembrance of the farmhouse, a shattered mirror lies in the hallway, to be trodden underfoot. It reflects light beautifully, but cannot yield a full image—a recognizable identity. "Who knows about these things?" Eiseley muses.

Who knows, sometimes in age, what one really is or if someone else—or alternately others—gazes from the eyes we imagine are our own? Even psychologists admit to the reality of multiple personality. [ASH, p. 268]

The pathos of identity is also pointed to by the complex symbol of Tom Murry. In Chapter 3, Eiseley cryptically refers to something important that happened when he was five years old. "You see," he says in a conversation with W. H. Auden, "there was a warden, a prison, and a blizzard. Also, there was an armed posse and a death" (ASH, p. 26). As the autobiography unfolds, Eiseley gradually recovers more of the buried memory. In Chapter 16, the reader begins to perceive the detail and significance of the howling Nebraska March blizzard, Eiseley's father reading the newspaper by the kerosene lamplight, and his remembered comment: "They won't make it." The full story is told only in the penultimate chapter, as Eiseley reads of the events on newspaper microfilm: the brutality and torture of prison life, Tom Murry's gang's breakout, the final inevitable violence as the escapees are caught. But the phrase "They never made it" and the oft-remembered image of the drifting snow and howling winds have both been reiterated so frequently that the prison fugitive becomes almost totally identified with Eiseley. So the final detail fits perfectly: Eiseley says he had written "Tom Murry" on the signout slip for the newspaper microfilm but changed his mind and filled out another with "Loren Eiseley" because a voice whispered, "The other alias is better" (ASH, p. 257).

The brilliant final chapter of *All the Strange Hours* centers on an imaginary dialogue between Eiseley and death, which is personified as a dice player. A youthful drifter—Eiseley himself—appears as a third character. The Bergmanesque piece is "the story of a dream," and thus identities merge and overlap, as do time and memory sequences. At one point, Eiseley is Tom Murry, standing "alone on a western hilltop in the falling snow of a blizzard that would never cease so long as the world remained" (ASH, p. 264). But he comes to see that he must transcend his identification with the tragic Murry, whose death Eiseley had embraced as his own when only a child of five. Murry's unplacated ghost keeps Eiseley in the game, attached to the wheel of existence.

The problem, intimates Eiseley, is identification itself, especially identification with things human. "I did not care to be a man, only a being," he realizes. Tom Murry "had died as a hunted man yet still defined as human" (ASH, p. 266). The point is to be fully discharged from the guilts and obsessions of historical consciousness itself. "But in that greater winter where I sought retreat, Tom Murry could lead me no further. I would continue to fall and die to no purpose" (ASH, p. 266). Eiseley calls upon his beloved dog Wolf to "help me past that endless confrontation in the snow." Death will mean a release from "taxonomic definitions." An ice age will return to obliterate the human race with its proud aloofness from animal kindred. In the coming winter,

we would be no longer man or dog, but creatures, creatures with no knowledge of contingency or games. All the carefully drawn human lines would be erased between us, the snows deeper, the posse floundering, the dice cup muted in the Play-er's hand. [ASH, p. 266]

So Eiseley's symbols come to rest in an image-free plea for nullification. No longer dog or human, but crea-tures, "We would vanish together in an anonymous grey blur" (ASH, p. 266). Throughout the autobiography, he has intoned these words: *"Behind nothing, before nothing, worship it the zero."* The reference is to the time-obsessed Mayans, whose gods were numbers and whose great civ-ilization utterly vanished. In the ingenious Mayan count-ing system, huge numbers could be generated by moving the symbol for zero into different vertical positions. The Mayans dealt with time in enormous quantities; theirs was a calendrical society, and so colossal were their time vistas that they lost sight of the merely personal. Per-sonality, Eiseley hints, is resolvable into mere individ-uality. Individuality is but a mathematical convention, bare unity, which gains its significance only in relation to the sovereign zero, before which even death is pow-erless.[5]

Critic Francis Hart has developed a useful classification of autobiography.[6] The *confession*, he argues, is concerned with the truth of the self—its essential nature, its relation to reality. It is ontological, concerned with being as such. The *apology* wishes to "demonstrate the integrity of the self" in its relation to society. It is ethical, concerned with moral law. The *memoir* tries to show the historical dimension of the self. It is mainly cultural, concerned with "life and times." In this kind of scheme, *All the Strange Hours* must certainly belong to the confession. The book seeks to uncover the essential truth of the self. It refuses to discuss its bearing in society and hardly mentions historical events and its relation to them. Its stance is always relative to reality or to time in all its hugeness, not to the minuteness of particular personages or events.

The narrator of *All the Strange Hours* is aware of this peculiarity. He says that events of history had little importance in his life and that "animals outnumber by far the famous people I have met" (ASH, p. 152). The book is singular for its lack of names, places, dates. Given the chaos of the time in which Eiseley lived, the fact that only the Depression and World War II seem to have importance to the narrator is astonishing. There is no mention of the McCarthy era, Viet Nam, or the environmental crisis, all of which were of great importance in academia. National or international politics of any sort do not intrude. Eiseley seems to be totally apolitical and beyond the vicissitudes of the historical moment.

Eiseley's confession reminds one both of St. Augustine's self-revelation and the autobiographical novels of Thomas Wolfe. Like Augustine, Eiseley is convinced that the mysterious operations of memory reveal more than the mere contents of consciousness. Memory not only preserves us against time's ravages but also convinces us of a divine presence.[7] Eiseley, like Wolfe, is a lyrical poet of memory. Both writers are tormented by the strange, poignant beauty of lost pasts held in existence only by the attentiveness of a lonely memorist. Both see imagination as sustained by memory. Time, for Eiseley and Wolfe, is a massive force that ravishes precious human moments. Memory secures the insecure, holds the moment, stays the junk wagon between 14th and R streets.

What memory means to Eiseley and how it functions for him are illustrated by "The Palmist" in *All the Strange Hours*. The chapter begins, "You will die by water," words said to Eiseley by a palm reader. But the section's present is set much later, at a convention in Barbados,

as he remembers the prophecy while watching the spar-
kling blue Caribbean. That fortune becomes interwoven
with reflections on the three rings of memory—short-
term, immediate, and long-term—all of which are com-
plexly displayed in Eiseley's own memories from various
pasts. At low tide, as he walks far out among the sand
flats, he thinks of the immortality his footprints and the
raindrops on the sand might have were they to become
fossils. He thinks of how such fossil evidences, seized on
in the nineteenth century, "had proved earth carried her
own deep-ring memories of so simple a thing as a ten-
million-year-old rain" (ASH, p. 208).

His footprints trigger a memory of *Robinson Crusoe*,
the first book he ever read. A sighted shark and hurricane
warnings make him again recall the death prophecy, as
he seems to see beyond the sea wall a creature gesturing
toward him. The chapter ends with a fine surrealistic
reverie in which the library where he is working begins
to crumble, to moulder—collective knowledge vanishing
as the sea waters rise. His own death by water now
appears to mean death of his ideas. He tries to find his
books, remembers scenes of his youth, feels that his dead
dog is beside him. Finally he leaves the library, present
reality returns, and in the corner bar he drinks to his
lucky cast of the dice as a boy in the ruined Nebraska
farmhouse. Outside, "it was a cold night with starshine
and I had been far forward to the end. The palmist had
shown me the true death by water, but a sweetness
inexplicably lingered" (ASH, p. 213).

In the end, Eiseley's confession leaves us with a
vastly heightened appreciation for our own capacities for
experiencing life. Memory, time, and the mysterious par-
adoxes generated by human effort must now be recon-
sidered and approached with renewed awe. Eiseley's
loneliness, his tormented wrestling with identity, his de-

spair and nihilistic bitterness all somehow recede into a
larger picture. The remembrance of things past takes
precedence over the things remembered. We sense ourselves to be, like Eiseley, memory's willing victim. From
him, we learn how even in the failing days of old age
images mysteriously impressed into our minds as children surge forward and filter the present moment. His
"clairvoyant eye," says Eiseley, converts perceived ac-
tualities into startling amalgams of past, present, and
future. After such moments, he realizes that "something
has seized and held me . . . , created what is even more
real than what currently exists" (ASH, p. 150). Under
Eiseley's guidance, objective knowledge about evolutionary history becomes the stuff of vision. The deep evolutionary past, slumbering in brain and bone, asserts its
existence to his trained and receptive mind, stirring up
tremendous images of worlds without human beings. So
absorbed in the past is Eiseley that he feels himself to be
a reincarnated soul, not human but mammal—and perhaps reptile. Because he dwells in the fullness of past
reality, he would even have us experience our connection
with living water and the first parental amino acids.

Thus, although Eiseley's autobiography is "the excavation of a life," it is not only Eiseley's life that comes
to light but also the multiplicity of human and animal
lives of which he is composed. *All the Strange Hours* is
obsessed with the notion that other selves gain a curious
immortality in the mind. Not only parental figures but
also persons about whom we "care nothing" take up permanent residence in our memories. As if by destiny,
obscure and insignificant contacts assume major importance, cannot be shaken. More singularly, "We go away
and the other person stays eternally young, to be seen at
rare and sudden intervals on a far corner, or down a
pathway in the dark" (ASH, p. 150). The dead live vi-

brantly in the present, dominate it even, stalking the realm of half-awake thought. Eiseley never penetrated this mystery to the extent he wished. He saw it as a key to the nature of love and human sympathy, both of which had for him autonomous, involuntary qualities.

In *All the Strange Hours*, Eiseley develops the image of the "mental studio." It is a lovely and, telling image that indicates with a special exactness Eiseley's feelings about his own work, the nature of memory, and the relation of art to the personal past. Although lengthy, it deserves to be quoted in full:

In all the questioning about what makes a writer, and especially perhaps the personal essayist, I have seen little reference to this fact; namely, that the brain has become a kind of unseen artist's loft. There are pictures that hang askew, pictures with outlines barely chalked in, pictures torn, pictures the artist has striven unsuccessfully to erase, pictures that only emerge and glow in a certain light. They have all been teleported, stolen, as it were, out of time. They represent no longer the sequential flow of ordinary memory. They can be pulled about on easels, examined within the mind itself. The act is not one of total recall like that of the professional mnemonist. Rather it is the use of things extracted from their context in such a way that they have become the unique possession of a single life. The writer sees back to these transports alone, bare, perhaps few in number, but endowed with a symbolic life. He cannot obliterate them. He can only drag them about, magnify or reduce them as his artistic sense dictates, or juxtapose them in order to enhance a pattern. One thing he cannot do. He cannot destroy what will not be destroyed; he cannot determine in advance what will enter his mind. [ASH, p. 151]

Afterword

To anyone conversant with Eiseley's works, the omissions necessary in an introductory study such as ours will seem all too apparent. Because of space limitations, pieces that rank among Eiseley's classics have gone undiscussed. "The Brown Wasps," for example, is an exquisite meditation on how all intelligent creatures require secure, cherishable scenery as framework for their action—"a bit of space with its objects immortalized and made permanent in time" (NC, p. 229). "The Fifth Planet" (ST) is a fine short story in the Wilbur Daniel Steele tradition. We have given but scant attention to *The Mind as Nature*, Eiseley's famous 1962 lecture to the John Dewey Society; this remains much studied among American educators. About Eiseley's achievements as a book collector, Darwin bibliographer, and teacher we have said little. Nor have we considered Eiseley's increasing detachment from his own discipline in the last two decades of his life.

As the volume of commentary on Eiseley increases in the coming years, gaps like these will certainly be filled. And when they are, the issue of Eiseley's standing in American letters will be ready for a more final determination. From our early vantage point, however, some

predictions about the future of Eiseley's literary reputation are possible.

There can be no doubt that Eiseley will take his
place alongside Thoreau, Joseph Wood Krutch, Aldo
Leopold, Wendell Berry, Rachel Carson, and Annie Dillard, the great fashioners of the American natural-history
tradition. As Leopold pointed out in the 1920s, the modern naturalist essay must not only be aesthetically expansive, deeply personal, and attuned to the intense
interconnectedness of things. It must also be uncompro-
misingly accurate in a scientific sense. As we have seen,
Eiseley satisfied all these criteria. The most unique and
distinctive thing about Eiseley's contribution is, of course,
his thorough-going evolutionism. All the major natural-
history essayists of this century are evolutionists, but
none of them sounds the Darwinian waters to anywhere
near the depths reached by Eiseley. In effect, Eiseley is
the Marcel Proust of evolution, remembering the past of
the life of his species. There is a difference between
Eiseley's essay "The Flow of the River" and Krutch's
"Desert Rain". Both are wide-ranging meditations on the
mysteries of water in southwestern desert places, but
whereas Krutch's mind is thoroughly imbued with evolutionary ideas, in his piece evolution is a mere aspect
of the situation. For Eiseley, evolution is its innermost
reality.

Thus, future histories of the natural-history essay
will necessarily include a chapter on Loren Eiseley. Like-
wise, scholars writing on development in the art of the
scientific essay will need to devote much attention to
Eiseley's special achievement. Only a portion of Eiseley's
work deserves the label "naturalist," after all. "The Angry Winter" (UU), "Man the Firemaker" (ST), "The Long
Loneliness" (ST), and "How Flowers Changed the World"
(IJ) are primarily specimens of scientific exposition, bril-

liant elevations of the scientific article to literary heights. Here, the company Eiseley keeps includes Lewis Thomas, Jacob Bronowski, Rene Dubos, Alexander Petrunkevitch, Issac Asimov, and Michael Polanyi. "The Long Loneliness," for example, discusses John Lilly's famous research on porpoises. At one point, Eiseley adopts the porpoise's point of view, and, through a wonderfully imaginative exploration, shows that the porpoise's world is radically conditioned by this creature's inability to manipulate its environment. The porpoise's innocence is a function of its freedom from the tyranny of tools and the power they confer on their users. The reader of this article receives both instruction and delight; the literary and expositional motives have become perfectly unified.

That Loren Eiseley has made a signal contribution to the art of the essay is therefore beyond question. Working within the personal essay tradition of Montaigne, he has immeasurably enriched natural history, set new literary standards for the expository scientific article, and opened remarkable new pathways in the field of autobiography. And as a stylist and craftsman Eiseley has few peers in writing the history of science.

Curiously, however, Eiseley's ultimate place in American letters may be determined not so much by his books as by his editors. At present, all of Eiseley's books are in print; most are notable financial successes. In the relatively near future, the millionth copy of *The Immense Journey* will be sold. *The Unexpected Universe*, *All the Strange Hours*, *The Night Country*, and *The Star Thrower* continue to do well. Ironically, this sort of success may damage rather than boost Eiseley's reputation.

The Immense Journey contains a half dozen essays based on dated scientific material. The point of much of the polemic in *The Invisible Pyramid* will be lost on a new generation of readers who need no reminding that "West-

ern man's ethic is not directed towards the preserving of
the earth that fathered him" (IP, p. 69). Already committed to developing an environmentalist ethic, they need
to know how this ethic can best be inserted into the
public-policy arena. *The Unexpected Universe* and *The Firmament of Time* include some essays and lectures that are
not Eiseley's finest work. Like all romantics, Eiseley could
succumb to sentimentality, melodrama, and bombast.
These qualities are too much in evidence in "The Unexpected Universe" and "The Ghost Continent" (UU).
A tendency toward pettiness and reactionary conserva-
tism damages "How Human is Man?" (FT). Diffuseness
of focus and excessively florid language plague "The
Golden Alphabet" (UU) and "How the World Became
Natural" (FT).

The facts point to the need for something like a
portable Eiseley collection—perhaps along the lines of
the fine *Star Thrower* book. This volume would contain
fifteen to twenty of Eiseley's finest essays, allowing the
full measure of his achievement in this field to be appreciated. It would stand alongside *All the Strange Hours*
and the Darwin books. Conceivably, an additional volume of selected fictions and poems would complete the
canon. Thus winnowed, Eiseley's work could be seen for
what it is, a powerful and exact exercise of what Theodore Roszak has called "rhapsodic intellect."

For Roszak, Western culture requires a science
grounded broadly and deeply in the human personality.
To overcome the reductionism, emotional flatness, and
compartmentalization of our age, we need scientists open
to dream meanings, nature mysticism, myth, "symbolic
resonance," and metaphysics. A "sacramental vision of
nature" should replace the empirical, operational approach of skeptical science, says Roszak. Nature must be
apprehended "not as an independent domain of reality

but as a mirror reflecting a higher reality, a vast panorama of symbols which speak to man and have meaning for him."[1] Roszak especially urges a sympathetic return to the thought structures of alchemy. How curious that he fails to invoke the name of Loren Eiseley, that "alchemist of the heart" in whom rhapsodic intellect dwelt with such remarkable fullness.

Notes

Preface

1. *Survival Printout*, ed. Total Effect [Leonard Allison, Leonard Jenkin, Robert Perrault] (New York: Vintage Books, 1973).

1: Alchemist of the Heart

1. *Time*, 6 December 1971, pp. 107–108.
2. "The Poetic Achievement of Loren Eiseley," *Prairie Schooner* 51 (Summer 1977):111.
3. The publication information for all of Eiseley's works is noted in the list in the Preface, along with the abbreviation used when quoting; *All the Strange Hours* (ASH), p. 265.
4. Ward C. Goodenough, "Loren Corey Eiseley: In Appreciation," remarks delivered at memorial service, University of Pennsylvania, 9 November 1977, pp. 2–3.
5. Bob Lancaster, "Loren Eiseley's Immense Journey," *Today* (*The Philadelphia Inquirer*), 27 January 1974, p. 18.
6. "Loren Eiseley: Lengthier Biography" (unpublished autobiographical typescript), University of Pennsylvania Archives, Box No. 1, p. 3.

7. He published "Index Mollusca and Their Bearing on Certain Problems of Prehistory: a Critique" in the 1937 volume of the Philadelphia Anthropological Society, and "Pollen Analysis and its Bearing Upon American Pre-history: a Critique" in *American Antiquity*, 1939, both parts of his dissertation. Professor Speck negotiated with the university for the publication of the whole, but we find no evidence of its having been completed. Some time after the development of the carbon 14 dating method, Eiseley withdrew the thesis from circulation at the University of Pennsylvania Library, since his dating methods had now been superceded. From the abstract, though, one can gather that Eiseley put together materials from several disciplines—paleontology, archeology, etc.—and critiqued some new methods.

8. "Loren Eiseley: Lengthier Biography," p. 4.

9. Lancaster, p. 19.

10. "Loren Eiseley: Lengthier Biography," p. 1.

11. In 1947, Eiseley published his first science piece for the lay reader, entitled "The Long Ago Man of the Future." It was also featured in *Harper's*.

12. "Charles Darwin, Edward Blyth, and the Theory of Natural Selection," *Proceedings of the American Philosophical Society* 103, No. 1 (February 1959):94–114.

13. Here we must mention what can only be called Eiseley's obsession with money. In reading his correspondence one discovers that his response to any proposal—a new position, a film, a television appearance, a lecture—was what kind of remuneration he would receive. He negotiated with various universities about possible posts, then renegotiated with Penn. He turned down lecture invitations if the institution could not pay his rather high fees ($1500 plus expenses in the last years). He dickered with Penn about the possibility of staying on beyond the normal retirement age. In 1965 his salary was $25,000; he received also a full-time secretary for his literary endeavors. Then, of course, there were his royalties and lecturing fees. He worried excessively about money, remembering the Depression years

and the despair of poverty. For a considerable time, he had the care of both his mother and aunt as well as several members of his wife's family. He lived modestly in an apartment, did not own a car, and did not take extensive vacations. He spent money on rare books, works of art (he and his wife had an extensive collection), and on several charities. He left a sizable estate yet worried over whether it would be enough.

14. John Medelman, "The Immense Journey of Loren Eiseley," *Esquire*, March 1967, p. 45.
15. New York: Harper & Row, 1962. This long essay also appeared in full as chapter 13 of *The Night Country*.
16. Lincoln: University of Nebraska Press, 1963. A revised and substantially enlarged edition of this book was released in 1973 by Scribner's as *The Man Who Saw Through Time*.
17. "Academic Outlooks: Loren C. Eiseley," *The Eternal Light*, NBC Radio, Jewish Theological Seminary, October 3, 1965.
18. Loren Eiseley and Eliot Porter, *Galapagos: The Flow of Wilderness* (London: Sierra Club, 1968).
19. Susan R. Schrepfer, "Conflict in Preservation: The Sierra Club, Save-the-Redwoods League, and Redwood National Park," *Journal of Forest History* 24, No. 2 (April 1980):66.
20. E. Fred Carlisle, "The Poetic Achievement of Loren Eiseley," *The Prairie Schooner* 51 (1977):123–124.
21. "In the Red Sunset on Another Hill," *The Innocent Assassins* New York: Scribner's, 1973), p. 41.

2. Eiseley's Medium: The Essay

1. James M. Schwartz, "Loren Eiseley: The Scientist as Literary Artist," *Georgia Review* 31 (Winter 1977):856.
2. The Library of Congress method of cataloguing books provides no help here at all. James Schwartz has explained the matter graphically: "If one wished to read Eiseley's books, he first must find them—but not in the literature section of the library. With the exception of the books announced,

and therefore automatically classified, as 'poetry,' one must abandon the Library of Congress category for Language and Literature ('*P*') and seek elsewhere for Eiseley: journey to the *B*'s of Philosophy and Religion for *The Mind as Nature* and *The Man Who Saw Through Time*; go to the *C*'s of History for *The Invisible Pyramid*; search the *G*'s of Geography and Anthropology for *The Immense Journey*; probe the *R*'s of Medicine to discover *Francis Bacon and the Modern Dilemma* (notice that the later edition of this, *The Man Who Saw Through Time*, is classified as Philosophy); or travel to the *Q*'s of Science for *The Immense Journey* (again), *Darwin's Century*, *The Firmament of Time*, *The Unexpected Universe*, *The Night Country*, and Eiseley's autobiography, *All the Strange Hours*" (p. 856).

3. Montaigne, "To the Reader," *Essais* (Paris: Éditions Garnier Frères, 1962), I, 1: "Je t'asseure que je m'y fusse très-volontiers peint tout entier, et tout nud."

   The narrator in Robert Musil's much-praised *The Man Without Qualities* explains that an essay is "the unique and unalterable form that a man's inner life assumes in a decisive thought. Nothing is more alien to it than that irresponsibility and semi-finishedness of mental images known as subjectivity" (Robert Musil, *The Man Without Qualities*, trans. Eithne Wilkins and Ernst Kaiser [New York: Capricorn Books, 1965], Vol. I, p. 301).

4. Mary E. Rucker, "The Literary Essay and the Modern Temper," *Papers on Language and Literature* 11 (1975):320.

5. *Saturday Review*, 23 July 1932; quoted by Rucker, p. 323.

6. "No Essays, Please," *Saturday Review of Literature*, 10 March 1951, p. 35.

7. "Thoreau's Vision of the Natural World," afterword to *The Illustrated World of Thoreau*, ed. Howard Chapnick (New York: Grosset & Dunlap, 1974) reprinted in ST, pp. 222–234; "Walden: Thoreau's Unfinished Business," in ST, pp. 235–250; "Man Against the Universe," in ST, pp. 207–221.

8. W. H. Auden, "Concerning the Unpredictable," intro. to *The Star Thrower*, p. 15.

9. Kenneth Heuer, "Editor's Preface," *Darwin and the Mysterious Mr. X* (New York: E. P. Dutton, 1979), p. xi.
10. Other short stories are "Obituary of a Bone Hunter" (NC) and "Big Eyes and Small Eyes" (NC).
11. John Buettner-Jansch, "Review of *The Firmament of Time*," *American Anthropologist* 65 (1963):694.
12. Eiseley's abilities as a preacher were much appreciated in other quarters. Despite his unusually high fees, Eiseley continually received invitations to speak, especially from small church-related colleges. (Many of his honorary degrees were from such institutions.) Tellingly, Eiseley's voluminous fan mail included many letters from ministers who had used his material in their own sermons.

3. *The Message of* Darwin's Century

1. Conrad Phillip Kottak, *Anthropology: The Exploration of Human Diversity* (New York: Random House, 1978), p. 12.
2. E. Fred Carlisle, "The Heretical Science of Loren Eiseley," *The Centennial Review* 18 (1974):365.
3. Quoted by John C. Greene, *The Death of Adam: Evolution and Its Impact on Western Thought* (New York: New American Library, 1961), p. 15.
4. James M. Schwartz, "Loren Eiseley: The Scientist as Literary Artist," *Georgia Review* 31 (Winter 1977):857.
5. Frederick Elder, Letter to Loren Eiseley, 8 March 1968, University of Pennsylvania Archives, Box No. 3.

4. *Creative Time and the Community of Descent*

1. George Gaylord Simpson, *The Meaning of Evolution* (New Haven: Yale University Press, 1949), p. 62.

5. *The Second World of Human Consciousness*

1. Jacob Bronowski, *The Ascent of Man* (Boston: Little, Brown, 1973), p. 31.

6. Ordinary Miracles: Science and the Sense of Wonder

1. E. Fred Carlisle, "The Heretical Science of Loren Eiseley,"
   The Centennial Review, 18 (1974): 354–377.
2. The other essays in this series are "The Inner Galaxy"
   (UU), "The Laughing Puppet" (ASH), and "The Hidden
   Teacher" (UU).
3. The reader is directed to, unter alia, "The Great Deeps"
   and "The Flow of the River" (IJ), "How Natural is 'Natural'?" and "How Life Became Natural" (FT), and "The
   Last Neanderthal" (UU).

7. For The Uses of Life: Eiseley's Defense of Bacon

1. The original title was *Francis Bacon and the Modern Dilemma*.
   We refer here only to the 1973 version, *The Man Who Saw
   Through Time*. It contains the essay "Strangeness in the
   Proportion," which first appeared in 1971 in *The Night
   Country*.
2. Excellent general material on Bacon can be obtained in
   Fulton H. Anderson's *Francis Bacon: His Career and Thought*
   (Los Angeles: University of California Press, 1962). Eiseley
   relied heavily on an earlier work by Anderson, *The Philos-
   ophy of Francis Bacon* (Chicago: University of Chicago Press,
   1948).
3. Benjamin Farrington, *Francis Bacon: Philosopher of Industrial
   Science* (New York: Schuman, 1949).

8. Science and Will: On Loving the Failures of the World

1. Herman Melville, *Moby Dick*, quoted in E. Fred Carlisle,
   "The Heretical Science of Loren Eiseley," *Centennial Review* 18 (1974):358. In Part III of "Science and the Sense
   of the Holy," Eiseley sees Ahab as symbolic of the obses-
   sive, Faustian character of much modern science; Ishmael

is viewed pursuing the poet's way, "attempting to see all, while disturbing as little as possible" (ST, 199–200).

2. Carlisle, p. 359.
3. Carlisle, p. 374.
4. Carlisle, p. 368.

9. Eiseley Unleashed: Ventures in Surrealism

1. André Breton, *Manifestoes of Surrealism*, trans. Richard Seaver and Helen R. Lane (Ann Arbor: University of Michigan Press, 1969), p. 26.

10. All the Strange Hours: An Autobiographical Masterpiece

1. *The Poems and Plays of Robert Browning*, ed. Ernest Rhys (New York: E. P. Dutton, 1946), Vol. III ["The Ring and the Book"], Book VI, ll. 1646–48, p. 242.
2. The autobiographies of Vladimir Nabokov and William Butler Yeats warrant comparison with *All the Strange Hours*. They possess the same formal elegance, symbolic richness, and literary complexity that Eiseley sought and achieved. But such literary autobiographies are rare flowers in the vast garden of autobiographical writing.
3. "Review of *All the Strange Hours*," *New York Times Book Review*, 23 November 1975, p. 36. We do not mean to suggest that it is not useful to view autobiographies as specimens of fiction; among literary critics, such a strategy is entirely normal. The issue here is the extraordinary degree of fictionalizing pressure evident in *All the Strange Hours*.
4. Introduction to ST, p. 19.
5. Eiseley's poem "The Maya," in *Another Kind of Autumn* (1977), uses the lines quoted in *ASH* (pp. 6, 10, 12, 264) and explores his view of this civilization. "Ask that you sleep" (AKA) is another poem on the same subject. It is

likely that Eiseley was working on the AKA volume at the same time he was finishing ASH.

6. Francis Hart, "Notes for an Anatomy of Modern Autobiography," *New Literary History* 1 (1969–1970):491.

7. Eiseley's link to Augustine is apparent in the epigraph to Part III, which comes from one "Ruland the Lexicographer." These lines indicate Eiseley's fascination with the lore of alchemy, which was itself inspired by the neoplatonic philosophy espoused by Augustine: "The Alchemical meditato is an inner dialogue with someone who is invisible, as also with God, or with oneself, or with one's good angel" (ASH, p. 215).

Afterword

1. Theodore Roszak, *Where the Wasteland Ends: Politics and Transcendence in Post-Industrial Society* (New York: Doubleday, 1972), p. 406.

Bibliography

1. Works by Loren Eiseley

The Immense Journey. New York: Random House, 1957.

Darwin's Century: Evolution and the Men Who Discovered It. New York: Doubleday, 1958.

Charles Lyell. San Francisco: W. H. Freeman, 1959 (10-page pamphlet).

The Firmament of Time. New York: Atheneum, 1960.

Francis Bacon and the Modern Dilemma. Lincoln: University of Nebraska Press, 1962.

The Mind as Nature. New York: Harper & Row, 1962 (John Dewey Society Lectureship Series, no. 5).

Man, Time and Prophecy. New York: Harcourt Brace, Jovanovich, 1966 (Address at University of Kansas Centennial).

The Unexpected Universe. New York: Harcourt Brace, Jovanovich, 1969.

The Brown Wasps: A Collection of Three Essays in Autobiography. Mount Horeb, Wisc.: Perishable Press, 1969.

The Invisible Pyramid. New York: Scribner's, 1970.

The Night Country. New York: Scribner's, 1971.

Notes of an Alchemist (poems). New York: Scribner's, 1972.

The Man Who Saw Through Time (Rev. and enl. ed. of *Francis Bacon and the Modern Dilemma*). New York: Scribner's, 1973.

The Innocent Assassins (poems). New York: Scribner's, 1973.

All the Strange Hours: The Excavation of a Life. New York: Scribner's, 1975.

Another Kind of Autumn (poems). New York: Scribner's, 1977.

The Star Thrower. Ed. Kenneth Heuer. New York: Quandrangle, 1978.

Darwin and the Mysterious Mr. X. Ed. Kenneth Heuer. New York: E. P. Dutton, 1979.

2. *Articles by Eiseley* (excluding essays collected in book form—see Section 3 below)

"Autumn—A Memory." *The Prairie Schooner*, 1, 4, (October 1927):238–239.

and C. Bertrand Schultz. "Paleontological Evidence for the Antiquity of the Scottsbluff Bison Quarry and its Associated Artifacts." *American Anthropologist* 37 (April 1935): 306–319.

"Review of *Archeological Studies of the Susquehannock Indians of Pennsylvania* by Donald Cadzow." *Pennsylvania History*, 4, 1 (January 1937):64.

"Three Indices of Quaternary Time and Their Bearing upon the Problems of American Prehistory: A Critique." Unpublished Ph.D. dissertation, University of Pennsylvania, 1937.

and Frank G. Speck. "Significance of Hunting Territory Systems of the Algonkian in Social Theory." *American Anthropologist* 41 (April 1939):269–280.

and Frank G. Speck. "Montagnais-Naskopi Bands and Family Hunting districts of the Central and Southeastern Labrador Peninsula." *American Philoosophical Society Proceedings*, 85, 2 (1942):215–242.

"Archeolgical Observations on the Problem of Post-glacial Extinction." *American Antiquities* 8 (January 1943):209–217.

"What Price Glory? The Counterplaint of an Anthropologist." *American Sociological Review* 8 (December 1943):635–637.

"Indian Mythology and Extinct Fossil Vertebrates." *American Anthropologist* 47 (April 1945):318–320.

"Myth and Mammoth in Archeology." *American Antiquities* 11 (October 1945):84–87.

"The Fire-drive and the Extinction of the Terminal Pleistocene Fauna." *American Anthropologist* 48 (January 1946):54–59.

"The Long-Ago Man of the Future." *Harper's Magazine*, 194 (January 1947):93–96.

"The Fire and the Fauna." *American Anthropologist* 49 (1947):678–680.

"Early Man in South and East Africa." *American Anthropologist* 50 (January 1948):11–17.

and Sol Tax, Irving Rouse, Carl F. Voegelin, eds. *An Appraisal of Anthropology Today* (International Symposium on Anthropology, New York, 1952). Chicago: University of Chicago Press, 1953.

"Program on the Darwin Collection in the Library." *American Philosophical Society Proceedings*, 98, 6 (1954):449–452.

"Reception of the First Missing Links." *American Philosophical Society Proceedings*, 98, 6 (1954):453–465.

"The Paleo Indians: Their Survival and Diffusion." In *New Interpretations of Aboriginal American Culture History*. Washington, D.C.: Anthropological Society of Washington, 1955.

"Charles Darwin." *Scientific American*, 194, 2 (February 1956):62–72.

"The Enchanted Glass." *The American Scholar*, 26 (Fall 1957):478 ff.

"Neanderthal Man and the Dawn of Human Paleontology." *The Quarterly Review of Biology*, 32 (December 1957):323–329.

"An Evolutionist Looks at Modern Man." *Saturday Evening Post*, 230 (April 28, 1958):29, 120–125.

"Charles Darwin, Edward Blyth, and the Theory of Natural Selection." *American Philosophical Society Proceedings*, 103, 1 (February 1959):94–115.

"Francis Bacon." *Horizon*, 6 (Winter 1964):33–47.

"Darwin, Coleridge, and the Theory of Unconscious Creation." *Daedalus* (Summer 1965), pp. 588–602.

"Introduction," to *The Shape of Likelihood: Relevance and the University*, Ala.: University of Alabama Press, 1971.

"Futures: the Crisis Animal." *Science Digest* 77 (January 1975):74–76.

"If the Human Race Is to Survive into the Next Century." *U.S. News and World Report* 78 (3 March 1975):43–44.

"Welcome to Craneology." *Harper's Magazine*, 251 (December 1975):121–122.

"Strange Hours: Eiseley on Eiseley." *Science News*, 109 (14 February 1976):109.

3. *Collected Essays and Fictions* (alphabetized by title)

"The Angry Winter," in *The Unexpected Universe*.

"Barbed Wire and Brown Skulls," in *The Night Country*.

"Big Eyes and Small Eyes," in *The Night Country*.

"The Bird and the Machine," in *The Immense Journey* and *The Star Thrower*.

"The Brown Wasps," in *The Night Country*.

"The Chresmologue," in *The Night Country*.

"The Cosmic Prison," in *The Invisible Pyramid*.

"The Creature from the Marsh," in *The Night Country*.

"The Dance of the Frogs," in *The Star Thrower*.

"The Dream Animal," in *The Immense Journey*.

"Easter: The Isle of Faces," in *The Star Thrower*.

"The Fifth Planet," in *The Star Thrower*.

"The Fire Apes," in *The Star Thrower*.

"The Flow of the River," in *The Immense Journey*.

"The Ghost Continent," in *The Unexpected Universe*.

"The Ghostly Guardian," in *The Star Thrower*.

"The Golden Alphabet," in *The Unexpected Universe*.

"The Gold Wheel," in *The Night Country*.

"The Great Deeps," in *The Immense Journey*.

"The Hidden Teacher," in *The Unexpected Universe* and *The Star Thrower*. ·

"How Death Became Natural," in *The Firmament of Time*.

"How Flowers Changed the World," in *The Immense Journey* and *The Star Thrower*.

"How Human is Man?" in *The Firmament of Time*.

"How Life Became Natural," in *The Firmament of Time*.

"How Man Became Natural," in *The Firmament of Time*.

"How Natural is 'Natural'?," in *The Firmament of Time* and *The Star Thrower*.

"How the World Became Natural," in *The Firmament of Time*.

"The Illusion of the Two Cultures," in *The Star Thrower*.

"The Inner Galaxy," in *The Unexpected Universe* and *The Star Thrower*.

"The Innocent Fox," in *The Unexpected Universe* and *The Star Thrower*.

"Instruments of Darkness," in *The Night Country*.

"The Invisible Island," in *The Unexpected Universe*.

"The Judgment of the Birds," in *The Immense Journey* and *The Star Thrower*.

"The Last Magician," in *The Invisible Pyramid*.

"The Last Neanderthal," in *The Unexpected Universe* and *The Star Thrower*.

"The Lethal Factor," in *The Star Thrower*.

"Little Men and Flying Saucers," in *The Immense Journey*.

"The Long Loneliness," in *The Star Thrower*.

"Man Against the Universe," in *The Star Thrower*.

"Man in the Autumn Light," in *The Invisible Pyramid*.

"Man of the Future," in *The Immense Journey*.

"Man the Firemaker," in *The Star Thrower*.

"The Maze," in *The Immense Journey*.

"The Mind as Nature," in *The Night Country*.

"Obituary of a Bone Hunter," in *The Night Country*.

"One Night's Dying," in *The Night Country*.

"Paw Marks and Buried Towns," in *The Night Country*.

"The Places Below," in *The Night Country*.

"The Real Secret of Piltdown," in *The Immense Journey*.

"The Relic Men," in *The Night Country*.

"Science and the Sense of the Holy," in *The Star Thrower*.

"The Secret of Life," in *The Immense Journey*.

"The Slit," in *The Immense Journey*.

"The Snout," in *The Immense Journey*.

"The Spore Bearers," in *The Invisible Pyramid*.

"The Star Dragon," in *The Invisible Pyramid*.

"The Star Thrower," in *The Unexpected Universe* and *The Star Thrower*.

"Strangeness in the Proportion," in *The Night Country*.

"Thoreau's Vision of the Natural World," in *The Star Thrower*.

"The Time Effacers," in *The Invisible Pyramid*.

"The Unexpected Universe," in *The Unexpected Universe*.

"Walden: Thoreau's Unfinished Business," in *The Star Thrower*.

"The Winter of Man," in *The Star Thrower*.

"The World Eaters," in *The Invisible Pyramid*.

4. Selected Articles about Eiseley and His Works

Auden, W. H. "Concerning the Unpredictable." *The New Yorker*, 21 February 1970, pp. 118–125.

Baker, John F. "[Interview with] Loren Eiseley." *Publisher's Weekly*, 3 November 1975, pp. 10, 12.

Blum, Howard. "Loren Eiseley, Anthropologist." *New York Times*, 11 July 1977, p. 28.

Carlisle, E. Fred. "The Heretical Science of Loren Eiseley." *The Centennial Review*, 18 (1974):354–377.

————."The Poetic Achievement of Loren Eiseley." *The Prairie Schooner* 51 (1977):111–129.

Dobzhansky, Theodore. "Review of *The Unexpected Universe*." *American Anthropologist* 73 (1971):305–306.

Elder, Frederick. *Crisis in Eden: A Religious Study of Man and Environment*. Nashville: Abingdon Press, 1970. (Chapter III, "An Eloquent Prophet," is on Eiseley).

Flory, Evelyn A. "Auden and Eiseley: The Development of a Poem." *Concerning Poetry* (Western Washington State College) 8, 1 (1975):67–73.

Friedrich, Otto. "Review of *The Night Country*." *Time*, 6 December 1971, pp. 107–108.

Goodenough, Ward H. "Loren Corey Eiseley: Two Pieces in Appreciation." Remarks at memorial service and at dedication of Loren Eiseley Room. Unpublished ms., 1979, University of Pennsylvania Archives.

Greene, John C. "Review of *Darwin's Century*." *American Anthropologist* 61 (1959):519–522.

Gruber, Howard E. "The Origin of the Origin of Species." [Review of *Darwin and the Mysterious Mr. X*.] *New York Times Book Review*, 22 July 1979, pp. 7, 16.

Howard, Ben. "Comment [on *The Innocent Assassins*]." *Poetry* 126 (April 1975):44–46.

Krutch, Joseph Wood. "Review of *The Immense Journey*." *New York Herald Tribune Book Review*, 25 August 1957, p. 5.

Lancaster, Bob. "Loren Eiseley's Immense Journey." *Today* (*Philadelphia Inquirer*), 27 January 1974, pp. 16–20.

Medelman, John. "The Immense Journey of Loren Eiseley." *Esquire*, March 1967, pp. 44–50, 92–94.

Neal, Steve. "Loren Eiseley Dies." *Philadelphia Inquirer*, 11 July 1977, pp. 1A, 4A.

Olney, James. "Review of *All the Strange Hours*." *The New Republic*, 1 November 1975, pp. 30–34.

Ramsey, Roger. "Eiseley's Art: A Note." *Notes on Contemporary Literature* 3, 5 (1973):9–11.

Rhoads, Jonathan E. "Loren C. Eiseley." *The American Philosophical Society*, Yearbook 1978, pp. 73–77.

Rusher, William A. "A Scientist with Soul." *Philadelphia Inquirer*, 20 July 1977, p. 9A.

Schrepfer, Susan R. "Conflict in Preservation: The Sierra Club, Save-the-Redwoods League, and Redwood National Park." *Journal of Forest History*, 24, 2 (April 1980):60, 65–66.

Schwartz, James M. "The 'Immense Journey' of an Artist: The Literary Technique and Style of Loren Eiseley." Ph.D dissertation, Ohio University 1977. *DAI* 38:2795A.

_____."Loren Eiseley: The Scientist as Literary Artist." *Georgia Review* 31 (1977):855–71.

Stafford, William. "Review of *All the Strange Hours*." *New York Times Book Review*, 23 November 1975, p. 36.

Stahlman, William D. "Review of *The Unexpected Universe*" *Saturday Review*, 13 December 1969, pp. 38, 40.

Werkley, Caroline E. "Professor Cope, Not Alive But Well." *Smithsonian* 6 (August 1975):72–75.

_____."Report of Loren Eiseley Collection." Unpublished ms., revised September 1978, University of Pennsylvania Archives.

Index

RITTER LIBRARY
BALDWIN WALLACE COLLEGE
WITHDRAWN